Joseph-Olivier Coté

**Political Appointments and Elections in the Province of**

**Canada**

From 1841 to 1865

Joseph-Olivier Coté

**Political Appointments and Elections in the Province of Canada**
*From 1841 to 1865*

ISBN/EAN: 9783337072131

Printed in Europe, USA, Canada, Australia, Japan

Cover: Foto ©Suzi / pixelio.de

More available books at **www.hansebooks.com**

# POLITICAL
# APPOINTMENTS

AND

# ELECTIONS

IN THE

# PROVINCE OF CANADA,

## From 1841 to 1865.

EDITED BY J. O. CÔTÉ, N. P.,

AND CLERK IN THE EXECUTIVE COUNCIL OFFICE

Second Edition, enlarged.

OTTAWA:

PRINTED BY G. E. DESBARATS.

1866.

PUBLISHED

UNDER THE PATRONAGE

OF HIS EXCELLENCY THE RIGHT HONORABLE

# CHARLES STANLEY, VISCOUNT MONCK.

GOVERNOR GENERAL OF BRITISH NORTH AMERICA,

&c., &c., &c.

THIS SECOND EDITION, PREPARED AT THE REQUEST OF INFLUENTIAL
POLITICIANS, IS RESPECTFULLY INSCRIBED TO ALL WHO
TAKE AN INTEREST IN THE GOVERNMENT
OF THE COUNTRY.

OTTAWA, JUNE, 1866.

▼

# CONTENTS.

## 1841 to 1865.

| | PAGE |
|---|---|
| Governors General........................................................ | 1 |
| Attorneys General, Lower Canada................................... | 4 |
| " Upper Canada................................... | 5 |
| Solicitors General, Lower Canada................................... | 5 |
| " Upper Canada.................................... | 6 |
| **Receivers** General.......................................................... | 6 |
| Postmasters General...................................................... | 8 |
| **Ministers of Finance**..................................................... | 7 |
| Ministers of Agriculture................................................. | 6 |
| Commissioners of Public Works........................................ | 8 |
| Commissioners of Crown Lands........................................ | 8 |
| Provincial Secretaries and Registrars............................... | 7 & 11 |
| Superintendents General of Indian Affairs.......................... | 10 |
| Governor General's Secretaries......................................... | 9 |
| Adjutants General of Militia............................................ | 16 |
| Customs, Commissioners of............................................. | 11 |
| Auditors of Public Accounts............................................ | 10 |
| Surveyor General, Office of.............................................. | 10 |
| The Queen's Printer...................................................... | 15 |
| French Translators to Government..................................... | 14 |
| Executive Council, Alphabetical List of............................. | 18 |
| " Chronological List of.......................... | 21 |
| " Presidents of................................... | 3 |
| " as periodically constituted................ | 24 |
| " Offices held by the Members of............ | 26 |
| Legislative Council, Appointed Members of.......................... | 53 |
| " Elected Members of.......................... | 56 |
| " Speakers of.................................... | 3 |
| " Electoral Divisions........................... | 61 |
| " Contested Elections.......................... | 107 |

## CONTENTS—(*Continued.*)

|  | PAGES. |
|---|---|
| Legislative Assembly, Members of | 63 |
| " Speakers of | 3 |
| " Constituencies of | 84 |
| " Contested Elections | 108 |
| Special Council for Lower Canada, prior to the Union | 119 |
| Deputies and Chief Clerks in the Public Departments, viz : |  |
| Attorney General's Department, L. C | 13 |
| " " U. C | 13 |
| Receivers General's " | 12 |
| Postmasters General's " | 13 |
| Ministers of Finance " | 12 |
| Ministers of Agriculture " | 13 |
| Commissioners of Public Works | 12 |
| " Crown Lands | 13 |
| Provincial Secretary's Department | 12 |
| " Registrar's " | 12 |
| Adjutants General of Militia | 10 |
| Executive Council Office | 11 |
| Legislative Council | 14 |
| " Assembly | 14 |
| Clerk of the Crown in Chancery | 15 |
| Governor General's Aides-de-Camp | 11 |
| Parliaments and Sessions, periods of their duration | 2 |
| Statutes passed during each Session, number of | 15 |
| " reserved | 15 |
| " reserved and subsequently sanctioned | 16 |
| " reserved and not subsequently sanctioned | 17 |
| " sanctioned and subsequently disallowed | 17 |
| Judges of the Superior Courts in Lower Canada | 120 |
| Judge of the Vice-Admiralty Court " | 122 |
| Judges of the Superior Courts in Upper Canada | 122 |

# CONTENTS—(Continued.)

|  | PAGES |
|---|---|
| Chancellors and Vice-Chancellors, Upper Canada | 123 |
| Pensions to Judges of Superior Courts " | 124 |
| "        "        Lower Canada | 124 |
| Queen's Counsel appointed for Lower Canada | 125 |
| "        "        Upper Canada | 126 |
| Commissioners for the Revision of the Public General Statutes, L. C. | 126 |
| "        "        of the Public and Private "   U. C. | 126 |
| "        for the Consolidation of the Public Statutes, Lower Canada | 127 |
| "        "        "        "   Upper Canada | 127 |
| "        "        "        "   Canada | 127 |
| "        for the Codification of the Civil Law, Lower Canada | 128 |
| French Canadians appointed or elected, number of | 129 |
| Princes' Visits to Canada | 130 |
| Canadians holding titles of honor under the British Crown | 130 |
| Consuls, foreign, in Canada | 130 |

# Governors General of Canada.

## 1841 to 1865.

| NAMES. | FROM | TO |
|---|---|---|
| **Lord Sydenham**, Governor General.................. | 10th February, 1841, | 19th September, 1841. |
| Major General **John Clitherow**, Deputy Governor......... | 18th September, 1841, | 19th September, 1841. |
| **Sir R. D. Jackson**, Administrator. | 24th September, 1841, | 11th January, 1842. |
| **Sir Charles Bagot**, Governor General................. | 12th January, 1842, | 29th March, 1843. |
| **Lord Metcalfe**, Governor General | 30th March, 1843, | 25th November, 1845. |
| **Lord Cathcart**, Administrator.... | 26th November, 1845, | 23rd April, 1846. |
| Do. Governor General. | 24th April, 1846, | 29th January, 1847. |
| **Lord Elgin**, Governor General (¹) | 30th January, 1847, | 19th December, 1854. |
| Major General W. **Rowan**, Deputy Governor............ | 29th May, 1849, | 30th May, 1849. |
| Lieutenant General W. **Rowan**, Administrator during the absence of the Governor General.................. | 23rd August, 1853, | 10th June, 1854. |
| **Sir E. W. Head**, Governor General..................... | 19th December, 1854, | 24th October, 1861. |
| **Sir William Eyre**, Administrator during the absence of the Governor General......... | 21st June, 1857, | 2nd November, 1857. |
| Lieutenant General **Williams**, Administrator during the absence of the Governor General..................... | 12th October, 1860, | 22nd February, 1861. |
| **Lord Monck**, Administrator.... | 25th October, 1861, | 27th November, 1861. |
| Do. Governor General. | 28th November, 1861, | |
| Lieutenant General **Michel**, Administrator in the absence of the Governor General..... | 30th September, 1865, | 12th February, 1866. |

(1) Died on 20th November, 1863.

# PARLIAMENTS AND SESSIONS–
## PERIODS OF THEIR DURATION.

1841 to 1865 inclusive.

| | FROM | TO |
|---|---|---|
| FIRST PARLIAMENT...... | 8th April, 1841, | 23rd September, 1844. |
| 1st Session ...... | 14th June, 1841, | 18th September, 1841. |
| 2nd do ...... | 8th September, 1842, | 12th October, 1842. |
| 3rd do ...... | 28th September, 1843, | 9th December, 1843. |
| | | |
| SECOND PARLIAMENT.... | 12th November, 1844, | 6th December, 1847. |
| 1st Session ...... | 28th November, 1844, | 29th March, 1845. |
| 2nd do ...... | 20th March, 1846, | 9th June, 1846. |
| 3rd do ...... | 2nd June, 1847, | 28th July, 1847. |
| | | |
| THIRD PARLIAMENT...... | 24th January, 1848, | 6th November, 1851. |
| 1st Session ...... | 25th February, 1848, | 23rd March, 1848. |
| 2nd do ...... | 18th January, 1849, | 30th May, 1849. |
| 3rd do ...... | 14th May, 1850, | 10th August, 1850. |
| 4th do ...... | 20th May, 1851, | 30th August, 1851. |
| | | |
| FOURTH PARLIAMENT.... | 24th December, 1851, | 23rd June, 1854. |
| 1st Session, 1st part, ...... | 19th August, 1852, | 10th November, 1852. |
| 1st do 2nd do ...... | 14th February, 1853, | 14th June, 1853. |
| 2nd do ...... | 16th June, 1854. | 22nd June, 1854. |
| | | |
| FIFTH PARLIAMENT...... | 10th August, 1854, | 28th November, 1857. |
| 1st Session, 1st part, ...... | 5th September, 1854, | 18th December, 1854. |
| 1st do 2nd do ...... | 23rd February, 1855, | 30th May, 1855. |
| 2nd do ...... | 15th February, 1856, | 1st July, 1856. |
| 3rd do ...... | 26th February, 1857, | 10th June, 1857. |
| | | |
| SIXTH PARLIAMENT...... | 13th January, 1858, | 10th June, 1861. |
| 1st Session ...... | 25th February, 1858, | 16th August, 1858. |
| 2nd do ...... | 29th January, 1859, | 4th May, 1859. |
| 3rd do ...... | 28th February, 1860, | 19th May, 1860. |
| 4th do ...... | 16th March, 1861, | 18th May, 1861. |
| | | |
| SEVENTH PARLIAMENT... | 15th July, 1861, | 16th May, 1863. |
| 1st Session ...... | 20th March, 1862, | 9th June, 1862. |
| 2nd do ...... | 12th February, 1863, | 12th May, 1863. |
| | | |
| EIGHTH PARLIAMENT.... | 3rd July, 1863, | |
| 1st Session ...... | 13th August, 1863, | 15th October, 1863. |
| 2nd do ...... | 19th February, 1864, | 30th June, 1864. |
| 3rd do ...... | 19th January, 1865, | 18th March, 1865. |
| 4th do ...... | 8th August, 1865, | 18th September, 1865. |

# Speakers of the Legislative Council.
## 1841 to 1865.

| SPEAKERS | FROM | TO |
|---|---|---|
| Hon. R. S. Jameson............ | 10th June, 1841, | 6th November, 1843. |
| " R. E. Caron.............. | 8th November, 1843, | 19th May, 1847. |
| " P. McGill................ | 21st May, 1847, | 10th March, 1848. |
| " R. E. Caron............. | 11th March, 1848, | 14th August, 1853. |
| " Jas. Morris.............. | 17th August, 1853, | 10th September, 1854. |
| " John Ross............... | 11th September, 1854, | 19th April, 1856. |
| " E. P. Taché............. | 19th April, 1856, | 26th November, 1857. |
| " N. F. Belleau........... | 26th November, 1857, | 1st August, 1858. |
| " Jas. Morris............. | 2nd August, 1858, | 6th August, 1858. |
| " N. F. Belleau (¹)........ | 7th August, 1858, | 19th March, 1862. |
| " Sir A. N. MacNab....... | 20th March, 1862, | 8th August, 1862. |
| " A. Campbell............ | 12th February, 1863, | 12th August, 1863. |
| " J. U. Tessier........... | 13th August, 1863, | |

(1) Hon. Mr. Belleau was Knighted on 21st August, 1860.

# Speakers of the Legislative Assembly.
## 1841 to 1865.

| | FROM | TO |
|---|---|---|
| Hon. A. Cuvillier............. | 14th June, 1841, | 30th September, 1844. |
| " Sir A. N. MacNab....... | 28th November, 1844, | 24th February, 1848. |
| " A. N. Morin........... | 25th February, 1848, | 27th October, 1851. |
| " J. S. Macdonald.......... | 19th August, 1852, | 23rd June, 1854. |
| " L. V. Sicotte............ | 5th September, 1854, | 25th November, 1857. |
| " Henry Smith (²)........ | 25th February, 1858, | 10th June, 1861. |
| " J. E. Turcotte........... | 20th March, 1862, | 12th May, 1863. |
| " L. Wallbridge........... | 13th August, 1863, | |

(2) Hon. Mr. Smith was Knighted on 21st August, 1860.

# Presidents of the Hon. the Executive Council.
## 1841 to 1865.

| NAMES. | FROM | TO |
|---|---|---|
| Hon. R. B. Sullivan............ | 10th February, 1841, | 11th December, 1843. |
| " D. B. Viger ............. | 12th December, 1843, | 17th June, 1846. |
| " W. Morris............... | 22nd May, 1847, | 10th March, 1848. |

1 *

## Presidents of the Hon. the Executive Council—*(Continued.)*

### 1841 to 1865.

| NAMES. | FROM | TO |
|---|---|---|
| Hon. Jas. Leslie............... | 11th March, 1848, | 14th September, 1848. |
| " W. H. Merritt............ | 15th September, 1848, | 7th April, 1850. |
| " Jos. Bourret............... | 17th April, 1850, | 27th October, 1851. |
| " M. Cameron............. | 28th October, 1851, | 16th August, 1853. |
| " Jno. Rolph.............. | 17th August, 1853, | 10th September, 1854. |
| " Sir A. N. MacNab....... | 11th September, 1854, | 23rd May, 1856. |
| " P. M. Vankoughnet...... | 24th May, 1856, | 1st August, 1858. |
| " J. E. Thibaudeau......... | 2nd August, 1858, | 6th August, 1858. |
| " Sidney Smith............ | 6th August, 1858, | 6th August, 1858. |
| " Jno. Ross................ | 7th August, 1858, | 26th March, 1862. |
| " J. B. Robinson........... | 27th March, 1862, | 23rd May, 1862. |
| " T. D. McGee............. | 24th May, 1862, | 15th May, 1863. |
| " Isidore Thibaudeau...... | 16th May, 1863, | 29th March, 1864. |
| " I. Buchanan............. | 30th March, 1864, | 29th June, 1864. |
| " George Brown............ | 30th June, 1864, | 21st December, 1865. |
| " A. J. Fergusson Blair.... | 3rd January, 1866. | |

## Ministers of Agriculture.

### 1852 to 1865.

From the date of the formation of the Office of Minister of Agriculture, under Statute of 10th November, 1852, (16th Vic. chapter 11), the Presidents of the Executive Council were from that day, *ex officio*, Ministers of Agriculture, up to 20th March, 1862.

| | | |
|---|---|---|
| Hon. Sir N. F. Belleau........ | 20th March, 1862, | 23rd May, 1862. |
| " F. Evanturel............. | 24th May, 1862, | 15th May, 1863. |
| " L. Letellier de St. Just... | 16th May, 1863, | 29th March, 1864. |
| " T. D. McGee ........... | 30th March, 1864. | |

## Attorneys General for Lower Canada.

### 1841 to 1865.

| | | |
|---|---|---|
| Hon. C. R. Ogden ............ | 10th February, 1841, | 15th September, 1842. |
| " L. H. LaFontaine ....... | 16th September, 1842, | 11th December, 1843. |
| " Jas. Smith............... | 1st September, 1844, | 22nd April, 1847. |
| " W. Badgley ............ | 23rd April, 1847, | 9th March, 1848. |
| " L. H. LaFontaine ....... | 10th March, 1848, | 27th October, 1851. |
| " L. T. Drummond........ | 28th October, 1851, | 23rd May, 1856. |

## Attorneys General for Lower Canada—(Continued.)
### 1841 to 1865.

| NAMES. | FROM | TO |
|---|---|---|
| Hon. G. E. Cartier............ | 24th May, 1856, | 1st August, 1858. |
| " L. T. Drummond........ | 2nd August, 1858, | 6th August, 1858. |
| " G. E. Cartier............ | 7th August, 1858, | 23rd May, 1862. |
| " L. V. Sicotte............ | 24th May, 1862, | 15th May, 1863. |
| " A. A. Dorion........... | 16th May, 1863, | 29th March, 1864. |
| " G. E. Cartier........... | 30th March, 1864. | |

## Attorneys General for Upper Canada.
### 1841 to 1865.

| Hon. W. H. Draper........... | 10th February, 1841, | 16th September, 1842. |
|---|---|---|
| " R. Baldwin............. | 17th September, 1842, | 11th December, 1843. |
| " W. H. Draper........... | 1st September, 1844, | 28th May, 1847. |
| " H. Sherwood............ | 29th May, 1847, | 10th March, 1848. |
| " R. Baldwin............. | 11th March, 1848, | 27th October, 1851. |
| " W. B. Richards......... | 28th October, 1851, | 21st June, 1853. |
| " Jno. Ross.............. | 22nd June, 1853, | 10th September, 1854. |
| " J. A. Macdonald........ | 11th September, 1854, | 1st August, 1858. |
| " J. S. Macdonald........ | 2nd August, 1858, | 6th August, 1858. |
| " J. A. Macdonald........ | 7th August, 1858, | 23th May, 1862. |
| " J. S. Macdonald........ | 24th May, 1862, | 29th March, 1864. |
| " J. A. Macdonald........ | 30th March, 1864. | |

## Solicitors General for Lower Canada.
### 1841 to 1865.

| Hon. C. D. Day.............. | 10th February, 1841, | 20th June, 1842. |
|---|---|---|
| " T. C. Aylwin ........... | 24th September, 1842, | 11th December, 1843. |
| J. A. Taschereau, Esquire ..... | 21st August, 1845, | 21st May, 1847. |
| J. E. Turcotte, " ...... | 8th December, 1847, | 10th March, 1848. |
| Hon. T. C. Aylwin ........... | 11th March, 1848, | 25th April, 1848. |
| L. T. Drummond, Esquire..... | 7th June, 1848, | 27th October, 1851. |
| P. J. O. Chauveau, " ..... | 12th November, 1851, | 30th August, 1853. |
| Dunbar Ross, " ..... | 31st August, 1853, | 26th November, 1857. |
| John Ross, " ..... | 27th November, 1857, | 1st August, 1858. |
| C. J. Laberge, " ..... | 2nd August, 1858, | 6th August, 1858. |
| Hon. John Rose.............. | 7th August, 1858, | 19th January, 1860. |
| " L. S. Morin........... | 19th January, 1860, | 23rd May, 1862. |
| " J. J. C. Abbott......... | 24th May, 1862, | 27th May, 1863. |
| " L. S. Huntington........ | 28th May, 1863, | 29th March, 1864. |
| " H. L. Langevin ......... | 30th March, 1864. | |

# Solicitors General for Upper Canada.

## 1841 to 1865.

| NAMES. | FROM | TO |
|---|---|---|
| Hon. R. Baldwin ............ | 10th February, 1841, | 14th June, 1841. |
| " H. Sherwood............ | 23rd July, 1842, | 16th September, 1842. |
| " J. E. Small ............ | 26th September, 1842, | 11th December, 1843. |
| " H. Sherwood............ | 7th October, 1844, | 30th June, 1846. |
| " J. H. Cameron .......... | 1st July, 1846, | 10th March, 1848. |
| W. H. Blake, Esquire.......... | 22nd April, 1848, | 30th September, 1849. |
| J. S. Macdonald, Esquire...... | 14th December, 1849, | 11th November, 1851. |
| John Ross, " ...... | 12th November, 1851, | 21st June, 1853. |
| J. C. Morrison, " ...... | 22nd June, 1853, | 10th September, 1854. |
| H. Smith, " ...... | 11th September, 1854, | 24th February, 1858. |
| S. Connor, " ...... | 2nd August, 1858, | 6th August, 1858. |
| Hon. J. C. Morrison............ | 22nd February, 1860, | 17th March, 1862. |
| " J. Patton................. | 27th March, 1862, | 23rd May, 1862. |
| " A. Wilson............... | 24th May, 1862, | 10th May, 1863. |
| " L. Wallbridge............ | 16th May, 1863, | 12th August, 1863. |
| " A. N. Richards.......... | 26th December, 1863, | 30th January, 1864. |
| " J. Cockburn............. | 30th March, 1864, | |

# Receivers General, Canada.

## 1841 to 1865.

| | | |
|---|---|---|
| Hon. J. H. Dunn............ | 10th February, 1841, | 31st December, 1843. |
| " W. Morris............ | 2nd September, 1844, | 20th May, 1847. |
| " J. A. Macdonald........ | 21st May, 1847, | 7th December, 1847. |
| " F. P. Bruneau.......... | 8th December, 1847, | 10th March, 1848. |
| " L. M. Viger............ | 11th March, 1848, | 26th November, 1849. |
| " E. P. Taché.......... | 27th November, 1849, | 23rd May, 1856. |
| " J. C. Morrison.......... | 24th May, 1856, | 2nd February, 1858. |
| " John Ross............ | 3rd February, 1858, | 1st August, 1858. |
| " F. Lemieux............ | 2nd August, 1858, | 6th August, 1858. |
| " John Rose............ | 6th August, 1858, | 6th August, 1858. |
| " G. Sherwood............ | 7th August, 1858, | 26th March, 1862. |
| " J. Carling............ | 27th March, 1862, | 23rd May, 1862. |
| " James Morris.......... | 24th May, 1862, | 6th March, 1863. |
| " A. J. Fergusson Blair..... | 7th March, 1863, | 15th May, 1863. |
| " W. P. Howland.......... | 16th May, 1863, | 29th March, 1864. |
| " Sir E. P. Taché.......... | 30th March, 1864, | 30th July, 1865. |
| " Sir N. F. Belleau........ | 7th August, 1865, | |

## (1) **Ministers of Finance.**

### 1841 to 1865.

| NAMES. | FROM | TO |
|---|---|---|
| James Cary, Esquire, (L. C.)... | 10th February, 1841, | 31st December, 1841. |
| J. Macaulay, " (U. C.)... | 10th February, 1841, | 8th June, 1842. |
| Hon. F. Hincks, (Canada.)..... | 9th June, 1842, | 11th December, 1842 |
| " W. B. Robinson........... | 20th December, 1844, | 30th April, 1845. |
| " W. Cayley............... | 6th August, 1845, | 10th March, 1848. |
| " F. Hincks.............. | 11th March, 1848, | 10th September, 1854. |
| " W. Cayley.............. | 11th September, 1854, | 1st August, 1858. |
| " Geo. Brown............. | 2nd August, 1858, | 6th August, 1858. |
| " G. E. Cartier........... | 6th August, 1858, | 6th August, 1858. |
| " A. T. Galt.............. | 7th August, 1858, | 23rd May, 1862. |
| " W. P. Howland.......... | 24th May, 1862, | 15th May, 1863. |
| " L. H. Holton........... | 16th May, 1863, | 29th March, 1864. |
| " A. T. Galt.............. | 30th March, 1864, | |

(1) From the 4th May, 1859, the name *Inspector General* was changed to that of *Minister of Finance*, under the provision of the statute of 1859. (22 Vic. ch. 14.)

## **Provincial Secretaries.**

### **1841 to** 1865.

| Hon. S. B. Harrison, (U. C.)... | 10th February, 1841, | 30th September, 1843. |
|---|---|---|
| " D. Daly, (L. C.)........ | 10th February, 1841, | 31st December, 1843. |
| " " (Canada.) ...... | 1st January, 1844, | 10th March, 1848. |
| " R. B. Sullivan........... | 11th March, 1848, | 14th September, 1848. |
| " J. Leslie.............. | 15th September, 1848, | 27th October, 1851. |
| " A. N. Morin............ | 28th October, 1851, | 30th August, 1853. |
| " P. J. O. Chauveau....... | 31st August, 1853, | 26th January, 1855. |
| " G. E. Cartier........... | 27th January, 1855, | 23rd May, 1856. |
| " T. L. Terrill........... | 24th May, 1856, | 25th November, 1857. |
| " T. J. J. Loranger....... | 26th November, 1857, | 1st August, 1858. |
| " O. Mowat.............. | 2nd August, 1858, | 6th August, 1858. |
| " C. Alleyn............. | 7th August, 1858, | 23rd May, 1862. |
| " A. A. Dorion........... | 24th May, 1862, | 27th January, 1863. |
| " J. O. Bureau........... | 28th January, 1863, | 15th May, 1863. |
| " A. J. Fergusson Blair..... | 16th May, 1863, | 29th March, 1864. |
| " J. Simpson............. | 30th March, 1864, | 29th June, 1864. |
| " W. McDougall.......... | 30th June, 1864, | |

# Postmasters General.

## 1841 to 1865.

| NAMES. | FROM | TO |
|---|---|---|
| T. A. Stayner, Esquire | 10th February, 1841, | 21st February, 1851. |
| Hon. Jas. Morris | 22nd February, 1851, | 16th August, 1853. |
| " M. Cameron | 17th August, 1853, | 10th September, 1854. |
| " R. Spence | 11th September, 1854, | 1st February, 1858. |
| " Sidney Smith | 2nd February, 1858, | 1st August, 1858. |
| " M. H. Foley | 2nd August, 1858, | 6th August, 1858. |
| " J. A. Macdonald | 6th August, 1858, | 6th August, 1858. |
| " Sidney Smith | 7th August, 1858, | 23rd May, 1862. |
| " M. H. Foley | 24th May, 1862, | 15th May, 1863. |
| " O. Mowat | 16th May, 1863, | 29th March, 1864. |
| " M. H. Foley | 30th March, 1864, | 29th June, 1864. |
| " O. Mowat | 30th June, 1864, | 19th November, 1864. |
| " W. P. Howland | 24th November, 1864, | |

# Commissioners of **Crown** Lands.

## 1841 to 1865.

| Hon. R. B. Sullivan | 10th February, 1841, | 30th June, 1841. |
|---|---|---|
| John Davidson, Esquire | 23rd July, 1841, | 12th October, 1842. |
| Hon. A. N. Morin | 13th October, 1842, | 11th December, 1843. |
| " D. B. Papineau | 3rd September, 1844, | 7th December, 1847. |
| " J. A. Macdonald | 8th December, 1847, | 10th March, 1848. |
| " J. H. Price | 11th March, 1848, | 27th October, 1851. |
| " John Rolph | 28th October, 1851, | 30th August, 1853. |
| " L. V. Sicotte | 17th August, 1853, | 26th August, 1853. |
| " A. N. Morin | 31st August, 1853, | 26th January, 1855. |
| " J. Cauchon | 27th January, 1855, | 30th April, 1857. |
| " E. P. Taché | 16th June, 1857, | 24th November, 1857. |
| " L. V. Sicotte | 25th November, 1857, | 1st August, 1858. |
| " A. A. Dorion | 2nd August, 1858, | 6th August, 1858. |
| " P. M. Vankoughnet | 7th August, 1858, | 18th March, 1862. |
| " G. Sherwood | 27th March, 1862, | 23rd May, 1862. |
| " W. McDougall | 24th May, 1862, | 29th March, 1864. |
| " A. Campbell | 30th March, 1864. | |

# Commissioners of Public Works.
### 1841 to 1865.

| NAMES. | FROM | TO |
|---|---|---|
| *(Under Stat. 4 and 5, Vic. ch. 38.)* | | |
| BOARD. | | |
| Hon. H. H. Killaly, Chairman ⎫ | | |
| " D. Daly............ ⎪ | | |
| " S. B. Harrison.......... ⎬ | 21st December, 1841, | 3rd October, 1844. |
| " R. B. Sullivan.......... ⎪ | | |
| J. Davidson, Esquire........ ⎭ | | |
| NEW BOARD. | | |
| Hon. H. H. Killaly, Chairman ⎫ | | |
| " D. Daly............ ⎪ | | |
| " W. H. Draper......... ⎬ | 4th October, 1844, | 8th June, 1846. |
| " W. Morris............ ⎪ | | |
| " D. B. Papineau........ ⎭ | | |
| *(Under Stat. 9, Vic. ch. 37, &c.)* | | |
| Hon. W. B. Robinson, Chf. Com. | 22nd June, 1846, | 10th March, 1848. |
| " E. P. Taché............ | 11th March, 1848, | 26th November, 1848. |
| " J. Chabot............ | 13th December, 1849, | 31st March, 1850. |
| " W. H. Merritt......... | 8th April, 1850, | 11th February, 1851. |
| " J. Bourret............ | 12th February, 1851, | 27th October, 1851. |
| " John Young............ | 28th October, 1851, | 23rd September, 1852. |
| " J. Chabot............ | 23rd September, 1852, | 26th January, 1855. |
| " F. Lemieux............ | 27th January, 1855, | 26th November, 1857. |
| " C. Alleyn............ | 26th November, 1857, | 1st August, 1858. |
| " L. H. Holton............ | 2nd August, 1858, | 6th August, 1858. |
| " L. V. Sicotte......... | 7th August, 1858, | 10th January, 1859. |
| " John Rose............ | 11th January, 1859, | 13th June, 1861. |
| " J. Cauchon............ | 13th June, 1861, | 23rd May, 1862. |
| " J. U. Tessier............ | 24th May, 1862, | 27th May, 1863. |
| " L. T. Drummond........ | 28th May, 1863, | 23rd July, 1863. |
| " M. Laframboise........ | 24th July, 1863, | 29th March, 1864. |
| " J. C. Chapais........ | 30th March, 1864, | |

# Secretaries to the Governors General.
### 1841 to 1865.

| | | |
|---|---|---|
| T. W. C. Murdoch............ | 10th February, 1841, | 4th August, 1842. |
| R. W. Rawson............ | 5th August, 1842, | 20th January, 1844. |
| Capt. H. Bagot, Private Sec'y.. | 16th February, 1842, | 20th March, 1843. |
| " J. M. Higginson " " .. | 20th March, 1843, | 31st May, 1846. |
| T. E. Campbell............ | 31st March, 1847, | 30th November, 1849. |
| Hon. R. Bruce, (1)............ | 1st October, 1851, | 31st May, 1854. |
| L. Oliphant............ | 19th June, 1854, | 18th December, 1854. |
| Viscount Bury............ | 19th December, 1854, | 31st January, 1856. |
| R. T. Pennefather............ | 27th February, 1856, | 20th March, 1861. |
| Capt. F. Retallack, Actg. Secry. | 21st March, 1861, | 24th October, 1861. |
| Dennis Godley............ | 25th October, 1861. | |

(1) Died on 8th June, 1862.

# Adjutants General of Militia.

## 1841 to 1865.

| NAMES. | FROM | TO |
|--------|------|-----|
| F. Vassal de Monviel ......... | 10th February, 1841, | 12th March, 1841. |
| B. C. A. Gugy, Adjt. Genl. L. C. | 14th March, 1841, | 30th June, 1846. |
| R. Bulloch, " U. C. | 10th February, 1841, | 30th June, 1846. |
| Sir A. N. MacNab, " Canada. | 30th June, 1846, | 30th June, 1846. |
| Lt. Col. P. Young, " " | 30th July, 1846, | 26th July, 1847. |
| G. F. DeRottenburg, " " | 1st July, 1855, | 30th June, 1858. |
| | | |
| P. Young, Dep. Adjt. Gen., L. C. | 10th February, 1841, | 11th July, 1841. |
| D. A. McDonell, " U. C. | 1st July, 1846, | Died in June, 1861. |
| E. P. Taché, " L. C. | 1st July, 1846, | 10th March, 1848. |
| M. P. D. Laterrière, " " | 5th June, 1848, | 23rd June, 1848. |
| A. De Salaberry, " " | 26th June, 1848. | |
| J. R. Nash " U. C | 1st January, 1862. | 31st August, 1862. |
| Walker Powell, " U. C. | 1st September, 1862. | |

# Superintendents General of Indian Affairs.

## 1841 to 1865.

The Governors General's Secretaries have held the office of Superintendents General of Indian Affairs, under Commissions from the Imperial Government, up to the 13th October, 1860, from which period the Commissioners of Crown Lands are *ex officio* Superintendents General of Indian Affairs, under the provisions of Provincial Statute, 23 Vic. ch. 151.

# Auditor of Public Accounts.

| | | |
|--------|------|-----|
| John Langton, Auditor ........ | 9th October, 1855, | ——— |
| Hon. J. Simpson, Asst. Auditor. | — August, 1864. | ——— |

# Surveyor General, Canada.

| | | |
|--------|------|-----|
| Thos. Parke, Surveyor Genl. (1). | 7th June, 1841, | 16th March, 1845. |
| Jos. Bouchette, Dy., " .... | 10th February, 1841. | 16th March, 1845. |

(1). The Office of Surveyor General was abolished on 17th March, 1845, by authority of Statute.

## (1) Provincial Registrars.

| NAMES. | FROM | TO |
|---|---|---|
| R. A. Tucker ................... | 10th February, 1841. | 9th January, 1851. |

(1). Under Statute of 1846, (9 Vic. ch. 114), the Provincial Secretary is to be ex officio Provincial Registrar after the demise of Mr. Tucker.

## Commissioners of Customs.

| | | |
|---|---|---|
| J. W. Dunscomb ............. | January, 1844, | 17th March, 1851. |
| R. S. M. Bouchette........... | 18th March, 1851. | |

## Provincial Aides-de-Camp to the Governor General.

| | | |
|---|---|---|
| F. G. Heriot ................. | 10th February, 1841, | 22nd November, 1841. |
| E. W. R. Antrobus ........... | 1st October, 1841, | 30th September, 1852. |
| L. G. Irvine................. | 1st November, 1852. | |

## Deputies and Assistants in the Government Offices.

### 1841 to 1865.

### Executive Council Office.

| | | |
|---|---|---|
| G. H. Ryland, Clerk.......... | 10th February, 1841, | 12th October, 1842. |
| E. Parent................... | 13th October, 1842, | 19th May, 1847. |
| J. Joseph.................... | 20th May, 1847 ..... | 26th May, 1851. |
| W. H. Lee ................. | 28th November, 1850, | |
| W. H. Lee, Assistant Clerk.... | 10th February, 1841 . | 25th November, 1850. |
| W. A. Himsworth, Con. Clerk.. | 28th November, 1853, | |

## Provincial Secretary's Office.

| NAMES. | FROM | TO |
|---|---|---|
| C. Dunkin, Ass't. Secr'y. L. C.. | 1st January, 1842, | 19th May, 1847. |
| E. Parent, " " " | 20th May, 1847, | |
| J. Hopkirk, " " U. C... | 1st January, 1842, | 16th December, 1846 |
| E. A. Meredith, " " | 20th May, 1847. | |

## Provincial Registrar's Office.

| T. Amiot, Deputy Registrar.... | 7th January, 1851, | 17th December, 1858 |
|---|---|---|
| W. Kent, " " .... | 29th October, 1858, | Died, 27th Feb. 1865. |
| G. H. Lane, " " .... | 1st March, 1865, | |

## Minister of Finance's Office.

| Jos. Cary, Dep. Min. of Fin.... | 1st January, 1842. | 31st August, 1863. |
|---|---|---|
| Wm. Dickinson, " " .... | 1st September, 1863. | 31st August, 1863. |

## Receiver General's Office.

| B. Turquand, Rec'r. General... | 1st January, 1844, | 1st September, 1844 |
|---|---|---|
| " Dep. Rec'r. Gen.. | 1st July, 1847, | 8th December, 1848 |
| T. D. Harington " " .. | 17th May, 1858, | |

## Public Works Department.

| S. Keefer, Deputy Com........ | 6th May, 1859, | 7th March, 1864. |
|---|---|---|
| T. Trudeau, " " ........ | 8th March, 1864, | |
| T. A. Begly, Secretary........ | 10th February, 1841, | 31st October, 1858. |
| T. Trudeau, " ........ | 13th December, 1859, | 7th March, 1864. |
| F. Braun, " ........ | 8th March, 1864, | |

## Attorney General's Office—Lower Canada.

| NAMES. | FROM | TO |
|---|---|---|
| J. Monk, Chief Clerk......... | 10th February, 1841, | 6th March, 1848. |
| R. S. M. Bouchette, Clerk..... | 16th March, 1848, | 17th March, 1851. |
| G. Futvoye, Per. Cl'k. Law Dep. | 2nd May, 1851, | |

## Attorney General's Office—Upper Canada.

| NAMES. | FROM | TO |
|---|---|---|
| T. Galt, L. Hayden, J. Popham, } Chief Clerks.... | 10th February, 1841, | 27th March, 1848. |
| M. A. Higgins, Clerk.......... | 28th March, 1848, | 28th May, 1854. |
| R. A. Harrison, "  .......... | 10th September, 1854, | 28th February, 1856. |
| H. Bernard, Secretary......... | 15th February, 1856, | |

## Crown Lands Department.

| NAMES. | FROM | TO |
|---|---|---|
| T. Boutillier, Asst. Com....... | 19th August, 1841, | 20th April, 1856. |
| A. Russell, "  " ....... | 18th July, 1857, | |
| J. Bouchette, Dy. Surveyor Gen. | 18th July, 1857, | |

## Postmaster General's Office.

| NAMES. | FROM | TO |
|---|---|---|
| W. H. Griffin, Secretary....... | 1st April, 1851, | 9th June, 1857. |
| "   "   Deputy......... | 10th June, 1857, | |

## Bureau of Agriculture and Statistics.

| NAMES. | FROM | TO |
|---|---|---|
| W. C. Crofton, Secretary...... | 1st January, 1849, | 31st March, 1853. |
| W. Hutton, "  ...... | 1st April, 1853, | — July, 1861. |
| J. C. Taché, Depy. Min. of Agri. | 11th August, 1864, | |

### French Translator to Government.

| NAMES. | FROM | TO |
| --- | --- | --- |
| T. Amiot.................... | 17th December, 1844, | 31st December, 1850. |

## Chief Officers, Legislative Council.

### 1841 to 1865.

| NAMES. | FROM | TO |
| --- | --- | --- |
| J. FitzGibbon, Clerk........ | 10th June, 1841, | 30th June, 1846. |
| C. E. DeLery, " ........ | 2nd June, 1847, | 31st March, 1850. |
| J. F. Taylor, " ........ | 1st July, 1850, | |
| C. E. DeLery, Asst. " ........ | 14th June, 1841, | 1st June, 1847. |
| J. F. Taylor, " " ........ | 14th June, 1841, | 30th June, 1850. |
| R. Lemoine, " " ........ | 1st July, 1850, | |
| R. Armour, Law Clerk....... | 14th June, 1841, | 30th September, 1845. |
| E. L. Montizambert " ....... | 1st April, 1846, | |
| F. S. Jarvis, Usher of Black Rod. | 10th June, 1841, | 21st June, 1852. |
| R. Kimber, " " " | 12th July, 1852, | |
| L. O. Vallerand, Sergeant-at-Arms ................... | 16th August, 1841, | Died on 3rd November, 1864. |
| O. C. Fortier, Sergeant-at-Arms. | 18th January, 1865, | |
| Rev. A. W. Adamson, Chaplain and Librarian............ | 15th June, 1841, | |

## Chief Officers, Legislative Assembly.

### 1841 to 1865.

| NAMES. | FROM | TO |
| --- | --- | --- |
| W. B. Lindsay, Clerk......... | 14th June, 1841, | Died 15th May, 1862. |
| W. B. Lindsay, Junior, Clerk... | 16th May, 1862, | |
| G. B. Faribault, Asst. " ... | 14th June, 1841, | 8th May, 1855. |
| W. B. Lindsay, Jnr. " " ... | 9th May, 1855, | 15th May, 1862. |
| G. W. Wicksteed, Law Clerk.. | 14th June, 1841, | |
| G. K. Chisholm, Sergeant-at-Arms ................... | 10th June, 1841, | 14th June, 1854. |
| D. W. Macdonell, Sergeant-at-Arms.................... | 15th June, 1854, | |
| J. Brewer, Librarian.......... | 14th June, 1841, | 18th September, 1841. |
| W. Winder, " ......... | 19th September, 1841, | 30th March, 1856. |
| Alpheus Todd, " ......... | 31st March, 1856, | |
| " " Asst. Librarian.. | 19th September, 1841, | 30th March, 1856. |
| A. G. Lajoie, " " .. | 31st March, 1856, | |

## Clerk of Crown in Chancery.

| NAMES. | FROM | TO |
|---|---|---|
| Thos. Amiot............... | 10th February, 1841, | 31st December, 1841. |
| F. Fortier ................ | 1st February, 1842, | 20th August, 1858. |
| L. R. Fortier.............. | 21st August, 1858, | 3rd January, 1865. |
| E. J. Langevin............ | 4th January, 1865, | |

## The Queen's Printers.
### 1841 to 1865.

| | | |
|---|---|---|
| Derbishire & Desbarats........ | 29th September, 1841, | 27th March, 1863. |
| Desbarats & Cameron.......... | 20th April, 1863, | 12th November, 1864. |
| M. Cameron.................. | — November, 1864, | |

### Number of Bills passed by the Legislature of Canada,
### From 1841 to 1865, inclusive.

| Years. | Bills. | Years. | Bills. | Years. | Bills. | Years. | Bills. |
|---|---|---|---|---|---|---|---|
| 1841 | 115 | 1848 | 18 | 1856 | 343 | 1862 | 110 |
| 1842 | 34 | 1849 | 206 | 1857 | 228 | 1863 | 164 |
| 1843 | 77 | 1850 | 145 | 1858 | 163 | 1864 | 174 |
| 1844–5 | 114 | 1851 | 182 | 1859 | 133 | 1865 | 196 |
| 1846 | 125 | 1852–3 | 265 | 1860 | 151 | | |
| 1847 | 136 | 1854–5 | 251 | 1861 | 141 | | 4,208 Average per session 163 Bills. |

### Number of Bills reserved for the signification of Her Majesty's
### pleasure thereon.

| Years. | Bills. | Years. | Bills. | Years. | Bills. | Years. | Bills. |
|---|---|---|---|---|---|---|---|
| 1841 | 15 | 1846 | 10 | 1852–3 | 1 | 1860 | 1 |
| 1842 | 2 | 1847 | 13 | 1856 | 2 | 1861 | 1 |
| 1843 | 9 | 1849 | 6 | 1857 | 1 | 1862 | 1 |
| 1844–5 | 7 | 1851 | 6 | 1859 | 1 | 1864 | 1 |
| | | | | | | | 77 |

## Short titles of Bills reserved (62) and subsequently assented to.

1841.—4 & 5 Vict. ch.  88.—Beef and Pork Inspection.
    "    "    89.—Flour and Meal Inspection.
    "    "    90.—Board of Trade, Montreal.
    "    "    91.—Securities from Public Officers.
    "    "    92.—Board of Trade, Quebec.
    "    "    93.—Currency Act.
    "    "    94.—Bank, Quebec.
    "    "    95.—Bank of Upper Canada.
    "    "    96.—Bank of Niagara District.
    "    "    97.—Bank, City.
    "    "    98.—Bank of Montreal.
    "    "    99.—Banks, chartered.
    "    "   100.—Public Lands, disposal of.

1842.—6 Vict. ch. 31.—Foreign Wheat Act.
    "    "    32.—Church of England Temporalities, Quebec.

1843.—7 Vict. ch. 65.—Legislative Assembly Independence Act.
    "    "    66.—Banque du Peuple.
    "    "    67.—Bank of Niagara District.
    "    "    68.—Church of England Societies, Quebec and Toronto.

1844-5.—8 Vict. ch. 107.—Alien Act.

1846.—9 Vict. ch. 106.—High Treason.
    "    "   107.—Railway, Montreal and Kingston.
    "    "   108.—   "   Wolfe Island, Kingston and Toronto.
    "    "   109.—   "   Peterboro' and Port Hope.
    "    "   110.—   "   Hamilton and Toronto.
    "    "   111.—   "   Toronto and Lake Huron.
    "    "   112.—Suspension Bridge, Niagara.
    "    "   113.—Water Works, Quebec.
    "    "   114.—Civil List Act.
    "    "   115.—Banque des Marchands.

**1847.—10 & 11** Vict. ch. 111.—Seigniorial Tenure Act.
    "    "   112.—Alien Act.
    "    "   113.—Bank of Quebec **District.**
    "    "   114.—Bank of Quebec.
    "    "   115.—Bank of Montreal.
    "    "   116.—Bank, City.
    "    "   117.—Railway and Harbour, Woodstock.
    "    "   118.—   "   Bytown and Britannia.
    "    "   119.—   "   Carillon and Grenville.
    "    "   120.—   "   St. Louis and Province Line.
    "    "   121.—   "   Montreal and Province Line.
    "    "   122.—   "   Halifax.
    "    "   123.—   "   Toronto and Goderich.

1849.—12 Vict. ch. 196.—Railway, Toronto, Simcoe and Huron (Northern).
    "    "   197.—Alien Act.
    "    "   198.—Alien Act, Lower Canada.
    "    "   199.—Suspension Bridge, Queenston.
    "    "   200.—School Land Fund.

## Short titles of Bills reserved, &c.—(Continued.)

1851.—14 and 15 Vict. ch. 171.—Church of England Societies, L. C.
   "     "     172.—Suspension Bridge, &c., Fort Erie.
   "     "     173.—Civil List Act.
   "     "     174.—Salaries of Judicial officers and the Speaker.
   "     "     175.—Rectories Act.
   "     "     176.—Church of England Temporalities, Montreal.
1852-3.—16 Vict. ch. 267.—Divorse Bill, W. H. Beresford.
1856.—19 and 20 Vict. c. 140.—Legislative Council made Elective.
   "     "     141.—Church of England to meet in Synod.
1857.—20 Vict. ch. 227.—International Bridge.
1859.—22 Vict. ch. 132.—Divorse Bill, J. McLean.
1860.—23 Vict. ch. 151.—Indian Lands and property management.
1861.—24 " " 141.—Lottery Act, Caproel.
1864.—27 & 28 " 175.—Divorse Bill, J. Benning.

## Short titles of Bills (15) reserved and not subsequently assented to.

1841.—Haldimand Glass Works Company, Incorporation of.
  "  For the freedom of Elections.
1843.—Legislative Council Independence Bill.
  "  Secret Societies prevention Bill.
  "  Land Surveyors' Act, U. C.
  "  Market Block Vesting Act, Town of Niagara.
  "  Navigation of the St. Lawrence, Port of Quebec.
1844-5.—Divorse Bill, H. W. Harris.
  "  Alien Act, L. C.
  "  Ordnance Vesting Act amendment.
  "  Boundary of Beverley Township.
  "  For legal recourse against the Executive Government.
  "  Official Salaries Attachment.
1849.—Savings Banks Amendment Bill.
1862.—Ferry, New Edinburgh and Waterloo.

## Bills (2) sanctioned by the Governor General, and subsequently disallowed by the Imperial Government.

1847.—10 & 11 Vict. ch. 43.—Bytown Incorporation Act.
1859.—22 Vict. c. 16.—Foreign Ships Duty Act.

## *Alphabetical List of the Members of the Executive Council, From 1841 to 1865, inclusive.

| NAMES. | Age when appointed | FROM | TO | L. C. | U.C. |
|---|---|---|---|---|---|
| Abbott, J. J. C., Hon.. | 41 | 24th May, 1862, | 27th May, 1863, | " | ... |
| Alleyn, Charles, " .. | 40 | 26th Nov., 1857, | 29th July, 1858, | " | ... |
| " " " .. | .. | 6th August, 1858, | 23rd May, 1862, | " | ... |
| Aylwin, T. C. " .. | .. | 24th Sept., 1842, | 27th Nov., 1843, | " | ... |
| " " " .. | .. | 11th March, 1848, | 25th April, 1848, | " | ... |
| Badgley, Wm. " .. | 46 | 23rd April, 1847, | 10th March, 1848, | " | ... |
| Baldwin, R. " .. | 37 | 13th Feb., 1841, | 13th June, 1841, | ... | " |
| " " " .. | .. | 16th Sept., 1842, | 27th Nov., 1843, | ... | " |
| " " " .. | .. | 11th March, 1848, | 27th Oct., 1851, | ... | " |
| Belleau, N. F., Hon. Sir | 49 | 26th Nov. 1857, | 29th July, 1858, | " | ... |
| " " " .. | .. | 6th August, 1858, | 23rd May, 1862, | " | ... |
| " " " .. | .. | 7th August, 1865, | ——— | " | ... |
| Blair, A. J. F. " .. | 48 | 7th March, 1863, | 29th March, 1864, | ... | " |
| Bourret, Jos. " .. | .. | 17th April, 1850, | 27th Oct., 1851, | " | ... |
| Brown, George " .. | 40 | 2nd Aug., 1858, | 4th Aug., 1858, | ... | " |
| " " " .. | .. | 30th June, 1864, | 21st Dec., 1865, | ... | " |
| Bruneau, F. P. " .. | .. | 8th Dec., 1847, | 10th March, 1848, | " | ... |
| Buchanan, I. " .. | 54 | 30th March, 1864, | 29th June, 1864.. | ... | " |
| Burean, J. O. " .. | .. | 28th Jan., 1863, | 15th May, 1863, | " | ... |
| Cameron, J. H. " .. | 30 | 22nd May, 1847, | 10th March, 1848, | ... | " |
| Cameron, M. " .. | 40 | 11th March, 1848, | 1st Feb., 1850, | ... | " |
| " " " .. | .. | 28th Oct., 1851, | 10th Sep., 1854, | ... | " |
| Campbell, A. " .. | .. | 30th March, 1864, | | ... | " |
| Carling, J. " .. | 34 | 27th March, 1862, | 23rd May, 1862, | ... | " |
| Caron, R. E. " .. | .. | 11th March, 1848, | 26th Nov., 1849, | " | ... |
| " " " .. | .. | 28th Oct., 1851, | 14th Aug., 1853, | " | ... |
| Cartier, G. E. " .. | 41 | 27th Jan., 1855, | 29th July, 1858, | " | ... |
| " " " .. | .. | 6th August, 1858, | 23rd May, 1862, | " | ... |
| " " " .. | .. | 30th March, 1864, | | " | ... |
| Cauchon, Jos. " .. | 39 | 27th Jan., 1855, | 30th April, 1857, | " | ... |
| " " " .. | .. | 13th June, 1861, | 23rd May, 1862, | " | ... |
| Cayley, Wm. " .. | .. | 6th August, 1845, | 10th March, 1848, | ... | " |
| " " " .. | .. | 11th Sept., 1854, | 29th July, 1858, | ... | " |
| Chabot, J. " .. | 42 | 13th Dec., 1849, | 31st March, 1850, | " | ... |
| " " " .. | .. | 23rd Sept., 1852, | 26th Jan., 1855, | " | ... |
| Chapais, J. C. " .. | .. | 30th March, 1864, | ——— | " | ... |
| Chauveau, P. J. O., Hon | 33 | 31st August, 1853, | 26th Jan., 1855, | " | ... |
| Cockburn, J., Hon.... | 45 | 30th March, 1864, | ——— | ... | " |
| Daly, D. " .... | 43 | 13th Feb., 1841, | 10th March, 1848, | " | ... |
| Day, C. D. " .... | .. | " " | 20th June, 1842, | " | ... |
| Dorion, A. A. " .... | .. | 2nd Aug., 1858, | 4th Aug., 1858, | " | ... |
| " " " .... | .. | 24th May, 1862, | 27th Jan., 1863, | " | ... |
| " " " .... | .. | 16th May, 1863, | 29th March, 1864, | " | ... |
| Draper, W. H. " .... | .. | 13th Feb., 1841, | 15th Sept., 1842, | ... | " |

* A blank in the column of dates indicates that the Officer was in office on 1st January, 1866.

# Alphabetical List of the Members of the Executive Council—(Continued.)

| NAMES. | Age when appointed | FROM | TO | L. C. | U.C. |
|---|---|---|---|---|---|
| Draper, W. H.  Hon. | .. | 12th Dec., 1843, | 28th May, 1847, | ... | " |
| Drummond, L. T.,  " | .. | 28th Oct., 1851, | 23rd May, 1856, | " | ... |
| "  "  " | .. | 2nd Aug., 1858, | 4th Aug., 1858, | " | ... |
| "  "  " | .. | 28th May, 1863, | 23th July, 1863, | " | ... |
| Dunn, J. H., Hon.... | .. | 13th Feb., 1841, | 27th Nov., 1843, | ... | " |
| Evanturel, F.  " .... | 41 | 24th May, 1862, | 15th May, 1863, | " | ... |
| Foley, M. H.  " .... | 38 | 2nd Aug., 1858, | 4th Aug., 1858, | ... | " |
| "  "  " ..... | .. | 24th May, 1862, | 15th May, 1863, | ... | " |
| "  "  " .... | .. | 30th March, 1864, | 29th June, 1864, | ... | " |
| Galt, A. T.  " .... | 41 | 6th Aug., 1858, | 23rd May, 1862, | " | ... |
| "  "  " | .. | 30th March, 1864, | | " | ... |
| Harrison, S. B.  " .... | .. | 13th Feb., 1841, | 30th Sept., 1843, | ... | " |
| Hincks, F.  " .... | .. | 9th June, 1842, | 27th Nov., 1843, | ... | " |
| "  "  " .... | .. | 11th March, 1848, | 10th Sept., 1854, | ... | " |
| Holton, L. H.  " .... | 41 | 2nd Aug., 1858, | 4th Aug., 1858, | " | ... |
| "  "  " .... | .. | 16th May, 1863, | 29th March, 1864, | " | ... |
| Howland, W. P., Hon. | .. | 24th May, 1862, | 29th March, 1864, | ... | " |
| "  " | .. | 24th Nov., 1864, | | ... | " |
| Huntington, L. S.  " | 36 | 28th May, 1863, | 29th March, 1864, | " | ... |
| Killaly, H. H.  " | .. | 17th March, 1844, | 27th Nov., 1843, | ... | " |
| LaFontaine, L. H. Hon. | 35 | 16th Sept., 1842, | 27th Nov., 1843. | " | ... |
| "  " | .. | 10th March, 1848, | 27th Oct., 1851. | " | ... |
| Laframboise, M.  " | 42 | 24th July, 1863, | 29th March, 1864. | " | ... |
| Langevin, H. L.  " | 38 | 30th March, 1864, | | " | ... |
| Lemieux, F.  " | .. | 27th Jan., 1855, | 25th Nov., 1857. | " | ... |
| "  " | .. | 2nd August, 1858, | 4th Aug., 1858. | " | ... |
| Leslie, Jas.  " | .. | 11th March, 1848, | 27th Oct., 1851. | " | ... |
| Letellier de St. Just, L. Hon............ | .. | 16th May, 1863, | 29th March, 1864. | " | ... |
| Loranger, T. J. J. Hon. | 33 | 26th Nov., 1857, | 29th July, 1858. | " | ... |
| Merritt, W. H.  " | .. | 15th Sept., 1848, | 11th Feb., 1851. | ... | " |
| Morin, A. N.  " | 39 | 13th Oct., 1842, | 27th Nov., 1843. | " | ... |
| "  " | .. | 28th Oct., 1851, | 26th Jan., 1855. | " | ... |
| Morin, L. S.  " | 28 | 19th Jan., 1860, | 23rd May, 1862. | " | ... |
| Morris, Wm.  " | 58 | 2nd Sept., 1844, | 10th March, 1848. | ... | " |
| "  Jas.  " | 53 | 22nd Feb., 1854, | 10th Sept., 1854. | ... | " |
| "  "  " | .. | 2nd Aug., 1858, | 4th Aug., 1858. | ... | " |
| "  "  " | .. | 24th May, 1862, | 6th March, 1863. | ... | " |
| Morrison, J. C.  " | .. | 19th April, 1856, | 1st Feb., 1858. | ... | " |
| "  "  " | .. | 22nd Feb., 1860, | 17th March, 1862. | ... | " |
| Mowat, O.  " | 38 | 2nd Aug., 1858, | 4th Aug., 1858. | ... | " |
| "  "  " | .. | 16th May, 1863, | 29th March, 1864. | ... | " |
| "  "  " | .. | 30th June, 1864, | 19th Nov., 1864. | ... | " |
| Macdonald, J. A.  " | 33 | 11th May, 1847, | 10th March, 1848. | ... | " |
| "  "  " | .. | 11th Sept., 1854, | 29th July, 1858. | ... | " |

2 *

## Alphabetical List of the Members of the Executive Council—(*Continued.*)

| NAMES. | Age when appointed. | FROM | TO | L. C. | U.C. |
|---|---|---|---|---|---|
| Macdonald, J. A. Hon. | .. | 6th August, 1858, | 23rd May, 1862. | ... | " |
| "    "    " | .. | 30th March, 1864, | | ... | " |
| Macdonald, J. S. " | 46 | 2nd August, 1858, | 4th Aug., 1858. | ... | " |
| "    "    " | .. | 24th May, 1862, | 29th March, 1864. | ... | " |
| McDougall, Wm. " | 40 | 24th May, 1862, | 29th March, 1864. | ... | " |
| "    "    " | .. | 30th June, 1864, | | ... | " |
| McGee, T. D. " | 37 | 24th May, 1862, | 15th May, 1863. | " | ... |
| "    "    " | .. | 30th March, 1864, | | " | ... |
| McGill, P. " | .. | 31st May, 1847, | 10th March, 1848. | " | ... |
| MacNab, Sir A. N.... | 56 | 11th Sept., 1854, | 23rd May, 1856. | ... | " |
| Ogden, C. R. Hon.... | .. | 13th Feb., 1841, | 15th Sept., 1842. | " | ... |
| Papineau, D. B. Hon. | .. | 2nd Sept., 1844, | 7th Dec., 1847. | " | ... |
| Patton, Jas. " | 38 | 27th March, 1862, | 23rd May, 1862. | ... | " |
| Price, J. H. " | .. | 11th March, 1848, | 27th Oct., 1851. | ... | " |
| Richards, W. B. " | .. | 28th Oct., 1851, | 21st June, 1853. | ... | " |
| Richards, A. N. " | .. | 26th Dec., 1863, | 30th Jany., 1864. | ... | " |
| Robinson, W. B. " | .. | 20th Dec., 1844, | 30th April, 1845. | ... | " |
| Robinson, J. B. " | 42 | 27th March, 1862, | 23rd May, 1862. | ... | " |
| Rolph, Jno. " | .. | 28th Oct., 1851, | 10th Sept., 1854. | ... | " |
| Rose, Jno. " | 37 | 6th Aug., 1858, | 12th June, 1861. | " | ... |
| Ross, Jno. " | 35 | 22nd June, 1853, | 18th April, 1856. | ... | " |
| "    " " | .. | 2nd Feb., 1858, | 29th July, 1858. | ... | " |
| "    " " | .. | 7th Aug., 1858, | 26th March, 1862. | ... | " |
| Sherwood, Hy. " | .. | 23rd July, 1842, | 15th Sept., 1842. | ... | " |
| "    " " | .. | 29th May, 1847, | 10th March, 1848. | ... | " |
| Sherwood, Geo. " | 47 | 6th Aug., 1858, | 23rd May, 1862. | ... | " |
| Sicotte, L. V. " | 40 | 17th Aug., 1853, | 26th Aug., 1853. | " | ... |
| "    " " | .. | 25th Nov., 1857, | 29th July, 1858. | " | ... |
| "    " " | .. | 6th Aug., 1858, | 24th Dec., 1858. | " | ... |
| "    " " | .. | 24th May, 1862, | 15th May, 1863. | " | ... |
| Simpson, J. " | .. | 30th March, 1864, | 29th June, 1864. | ... | " |
| Small, J. E. " | .. | 26th Sept., 1842, | 27th Nov., 1843. | ... | " |
| Smith, Jas. " | .. | 2nd Sept., 1844, | 22nd April, 1847. | " | ... |
| Smith, Sy. " | 35 | 2nd Feb., 1858, | 29th July, 1858. | ... | " |
| "    " " | .. | 6th Aug., 1858, | 23rd May, 1862. | ... | " |
| Spence, R. " | .. | 11th Sept., 1854, | 1st Feb., 1858. | ... | " |
| Sullivan, R. B. " | .. | 13th Feb., 1841, | 27th Nov., 1843. | ... | " |
| "    " " | .. | 11th March, 1848, | 14th Sept., 1848. | ... | " |
| Taché, Sir E. P. " | 53 | 11th March, 1848, | 25th Nov., 1857. | " | ... |
| "    " " | .. | 30th March, 1864, | 30th July, 1865. | " | ... |
| Terrill, T. L. " | .. | 24th May, 1856, | 9th Nov., 1857. | " | ... |
| Tessier, J. U. " | 45 | 24th May, 1862, | 27th May, 1863. | " | ... |
| Thibaudeau, J. E. " | .. | 2nd Aug., 1858, | 4th Aug., 1858. | " | ... |
| Thibaudeau, Isid. " | 44 | 16th May, 1863, | 29th March, 1864. | " | ... |
| Vankoughnet, P. M." | 33 | 24th May, 1856, | 29th July, 1858. | ... | " |
| "    "    " | .. | 6th Aug., 1858, | 18th March, 1862. | ... | " |

## Alphabetical List of the Members of the Executive Council—(Continued.)

| NAMES. | | | FROM | TO | L. C. | U.C. |
|---|---|---|---|---|---|---|
| Viger, D. B. | Hon. | .. | 12th Dec., 1843, | 17th June, 1846. | * | ... |
| Viger, L. M. | " | .. | 11th March, 1848, | 20th Nov., 1849. | * | ... |
| Wallbridge, L. | " | 47 | 16th May, 1863, | 12th Aug., 1863. | ... | * |
| Wilson, A. | " | .. | 24th May, 1862, | 10th May, 1863. | ... | * |
| Young, J. | " | 40 | 28th Oct., 1851, | 22nd Sept., 1852. | * | ... |

## List of the Members of the Executive Council, in the order of dates of Appointments.

## 1841 to 1865.

| NAMES. | FROM | TO | L. C. | U.C. |
|---|---|---|---|---|
| Hon. R. B. Sullivan........ | 13th Feby., 1841, | 27th Nov., 1843. | ... | * |
| " J. H. Dunn............ | " " | " " | ... | * |
| " D. Daly ............. | " " | 10th March, 1848. | * | ... |
| " S. B. Harrison ........ | " " | 30th Sept., 1843. | ... | * |
| " C. R. Ogden ......... | " " | 12th Sept., 1842. | * | ... |
| " W. H. Draper ........ | " " | " " | ... | * |
| " R. Baldwin ........... | " " | 13th June, 1841. | ... | * |
| " C. D. Day ........... | " " | 20th June, 1842. | * | ... |
| " H. H. Killaly......... | 17th March, 1841, | 27th Nov., 1843. | ... | * |
| " F. Hincks............ | 9th June, 1842, | " " | ... | * |
| " H. Sherwood.......... | 23rd July, 1842, | 15th Sept., 1842. | ... | * |
| " L. H. LaFontaine...... | 16th Sept., 1842, | 27th Nov., 1843. | * | ... |
| " R. Baldwin .......... | " " | " " | ... | * |
| " T. C. Aylwin......... | 24th Sept., 1842, | " " | * | ... |
| " J. E. Small.......... | 26th Sept., 1842, | " " | ... | * |
| " A. N. Morin.......... | 13th Oct., 1842, | " " | * | ... |
| " D. B. Viger ......... | 12th Dec., 1843, | 17th June, 1846. | * | ... |
| " W. H. Draper ........ | " " | 28th May, 1847. | ... | * |
| " Wm. Morris.......... | 2nd Sept., 1844, | 10th March, 1848. | ... | * |
| " D. B. Papineau ....... | " " | 7th Dec., 1847. | * | ... |
| " Jas. Smith ........... | " " | 22nd April, 1847. | ... | * |
| " W. B. Robinson ...... | 20th Dec., 1844, | 30th April, 1845. | ... | * |
| " Wm. Cayley ......... | 6th Aug., 1845, | 10th March, 1848. | ... | * |
| " Wm. Badgley ........ | 23rd April, 1847, | " " | * | ... |
| " J. A. Macdonald ...... | 11th May, 1847, | " " | ... | * |
| " J. H. Cameron........ | 22nd May, 1847, | " " | ... | * |
| " H. Sherwood.......... | 28th May, 1847, | " " | ... | * |
| " P. McGill............ | 31st May, 1847, | " " | * | ... |
| " F. P. Bruneau ........ | 8th Dec., 1847, | " " | * | ... |

List of the Members of the Executive Council, &c.—(*Continued.*)

| NAMES. | FROM | TO | L. C. | U.C. |
|---|---|---|---|---|
| Hon. L. H. LaFontaine..... | 10th March, 1848, | 27th Oct., 1851. | " | ... |
| " R. B. Sullivan......... | 11th " " | 14th Sept, 1848. | ... | " |
| " R. Baldwin .......... | " " | 27th Oct., 1851. | ... | " |
| " F. Hincks........... | " " | 10th Sept., 1854. | ... | " |
| " T. C. Aylwin ....... | " " | 25th April, 1848. | " | ... |
| " Jas. Leslie .......... | " " | 27th Oct., 1851. | " | ... |
| " R. E. Caron.......... | " " | 26th Nov., 1849. | " | ... |
| " J. H. Price.......... | " " | 27th Oct., 1851. | " | " |
| " L. M. Viger......... | " " | 26th Nov., 1849. | " | ... |
| " E. P. Taché.......... | " " | 25th Nov., 1857. | " | ... |
| " M. Cameron ......... | " " | 1st Feby., 1850. | ... | " |
| " W. H. Merritt........ | 15th Sept., 1848. | 11th Feby., 1851. | ... | " |
| " J. Chabot............ | 13th Dec., 1849, | 31st March, 1850. | " | ... |
| " Jos. Bourret.......... | 17th April, 1850, | 27th Oct., 1851. | " | ... |
| " Jas. Morris.......... | 22nd Feb., 1851, | 10th Sept., 1854. | ... | " |
| " A. N. Morin.......... | 28th Oct., 1851, | 26th Jany., 1855. | " | ... |
| " R. E. Caron.......... | " " | 14th Aug., 1853. | " | ... |
| " M. Cameron ......... | " " | 10th Sept., 1854. | ... | " |
| " J. Rolph............ | " " | " " | ... | " |
| " L. T. Drummond ..... | " " | 23rd May, 1856. | " | ... |
| " W. B. Richards ...... | " " | 21st June, 1853. | ... | " |
| " J. Young ............ | " " | 22nd Sept., 1852. | " | ... |
| " J. Chabot........... | 23rd Sept., 1852, | 26th Jany., 1855. | " | ... |
| " J. Ross ............. | 22nd June, 1853. | 18th April, 1856. | ... | " |
| " L. V. Sicotte ........ | 17th Aug., 1853, | 26th Aug., 1853. | " | ... |
| " P. J. O. Chauveau .... | 31st Aug., 1853, | 26th Jany., 1855. | " | ... |
| " Sir A. N. MacNab.... | 11th Sept., 1854, | 23rd May, 1856. | ... | " |
| " Wm. Cayley ......... | " " | 29th July, 1858. | ... | " |
| " J. A. Macdonald...... | " " | " " | ... | " |
| " R. Spence........... | " " | 1st Feby., 1858. | ... | " |
| " Jos. Cauchon......... | 27th Jany., 1855, | 30th April, 1857. | " | ... |
| " F. Lemieux .......... | " " | 25th Nov., 1857. | " | ... |
| " G. E. Cartier......... | " " | 29th July, 1858. | " | ... |
| " J. C. Morrison........ | 19th April, 1856, | 1st Feby., 1858. | ... | " |
| " T. L. Terrill ......... | 24th May, 1856, | 9th Nov., 1857. | " | ... |
| " P. M. Vankoughnet ... | " | 29th July, 1858. | ... | " |
| " L. V. Sicotte........ | 25th Nov., 1857, | " " | " | ... |
| " N. F. Belleau ....... | 26th Nov., 1857, | " " | " | ... |
| " Chs. Alleyn.......... | " " | " " | " | ... |
| " T. J. J. Loranger ..... | " " | " " | " | ... |
| " J. Ross ............. | 2nd Feb., 1858, | " " | ... | " |
| " Sidney Smith ........ | " " | " " | ... | " |
| " Geo. Brown .......... | 2nd Aug., 1858, | 4th Aug., 1858. | ... | " |
| " Jas. Morris.......... | " " | " " | ... | " |
| " L. T. Drummond ..... | " " | " " | " | ... |
| " F. Lemieux .......... | " " | " " | " | ... |
| " A. A. Dorion ......... | " " | " " | " | ... |

## List of the Members of the Executive Council, &c.—(Continued.)

| | NAMES. | FROM | TO | L. C. | U.C. |
|---|---|---|---|---|---|
| Hon. | J. S. Macdonald ...... | 2nd Aug., 1858, | 4th Aug., 1858. | ... | * |
| " | L. H. Holton ......... | " " | " " | * | ... |
| " | O. Mowat............ | " " | " " | ... | * |
| " | J. E. Thibaudeau ..... | " " | " " | ... | ... |
| " | M. H. Foley........... | " " | " " | ... | * |
| " | J. A. Macdonald ...... | 6th Aug., 1858, | 23rd May, 1862. | ... | * |
| " | G. E. Cartier......... | " " | " " | * | ... |
| " | P. M. Vankoughnet ... | " " | 16th March, 1862. | ... | * |
| " | L. V. Sicotte......... | " " | 24 Dec., 1858. | * | ... |
| " | N. F. Belleau ........ | " " | 23rd May, 1862. | * | ... |
| " | Chs. Alleyn .......... | " " | " " | * | ... |
| " | Sidney Smith ........ | " " | " " | ... | * |
| " | A. T. Galt ........... | " " | " " | ... | * |
| " | J. Rose.............. | " " | 12th June, 1861. | * | ... |
| " | Geo. Sherwood ....... | " " | 23rd May, 1862. | ... | * |
| " | John Ross............ | 7th Aug., 1858, | 20th March, 1862. | ... | * |
| " | L. S. Morin .......... | 19th Jany., 1860, | 23rd May, 1862. | * | ... |
| " | J. C. Morrison........ | 22nd Feby., 1860, | 17th March, 1862. | ... | * |
| " | Jos. Cauchon......... | 13th June, 1861, | 23rd May, 1862. | * | ... |
| " | Jas. Patton........... | 27th March, 1862, | " " | ... | * |
| " | J. B. Robinson ....... | " " | " " | ... | * |
| " | J. Carling............ | " " | " " | ... | * |
| " | J. S. Macdonald ...... | 24th May, 1862, | 29th March, 1864. | ... | * |
| " | L. V. Sicotte ......... | " " | 15th May, 1863. | * | ... |
| " | Jas. Morris........... | " " | 6th March, 1862. | ... | * |
| " | A. A. Dorion ......... | " " | 27th Jany., 1863. | * | ... |
| " | M. H. Foley.......... | " " | 15th May, 1863. | ... | * |
| " | Wm. McDougall....... | " " | 29th March, 1864. | ... | * |
| " | W. P. Howland....... | " " | " " | ... | * |
| " | U. J. Tessier......... | " " | 27th May, 1863. | * | ... |
| " | T. D. McGee.......... | " " | 15th May, 1863. | * | ... |
| " | F. Evanturel......... | " " | " " | * | ... |
| " | A. Wilson............ | " " | 10th May, 1863. | ... | * |
| " | J. J. C. Abbott........ | " " | 27th May, 1863. | ... | * |
| " | J. O. Bureau ......... | 29th Jany., 1863, | 15th May, 1863. | * | ... |
| " | A. J. Fergusson Blair.. | 7th March, 1863, | 29th March, 1864. | ... | * |
| " | A. A. Dorion.......... | 16th May, 1863, | " " | * | ... |
| " | L. H. Holton ......... | " " | " " | * | ... |
| " | O. Mowat............ | " " | " " | ... | * |
| " | I. Thibaudeau........ | " " | " " | * | ... |
| " | L. Letellier de St. Just. | " " | " " | * | ... |
| " | L. Wallbridge........ | " " | 12th Aug., 1863. | ... | * |
| " | L. T. Drummond...... | 28th May, 1863, | 23rd July, 1863. | * | ... |
| " | L. S. Huntington ..... | " " | 29th March, 1864. | * | ... |
| " | M. Laframboise....... | 24th July, 1863, | " " | * | ... |
| " | A. N. Richards....... | 26th Dec., 1863, | 30th Jany., 1864. | ... | * |
| " | Sir E. P. Taché....... | 30th March, 1864, | 30th July, 1865. | * | ... |

## List of the Members of the Executive Council, &c.—(*Continued.*)

| NAMES. | FROM | TO | L. | C. | U.C. |
|---|---|---|---|---|---|
| Hon. J. A. Macdonald...... | 30th March, 1864. | ———— | ... | | " |
| " G. E. Cartier......... | " " | ———— | | " | ... |
| " A. T. Galt............ | " " | ———— | | " | ... |
| " A. Campbell.......... | " " | ———— | ... | | " |
| " M. H. Foley.......... | " " | 29th June, 1864. | ... | | " |
| " T. D. McGee.......... | " " | ———— | | " | ... |
| " I. Buchanan.......... | " " | 29th June, 1864. | ... | | " |
| " J. C. Chapais........ | " " | ———— | | " | ... |
| " J. Simpson,......... | " " | 29th June, 1864. | ... | | " |
| " H. L. Langevin....... | " " | ———— | | " | ... |
| " J. Cockburn.......... | " " | ———— | ... | | " |
| " Geo. Brown.......... | 30th June, 1864, | 21st Dec., 1865. | ... | | " |
| " O. Mowat............ | " " | 19th Nov., 1864. | ... | | " |
| " W. McDougall........ | " " | ———— | ... | | " |
| " W. P. Howland....... | 24th Nov., 1864, | ———— | ... | | " |
| " Sir N. F. Belleau ..... | 7th Aug., 1865, | ———— | | " | ... |
| " A. J. F. Blair........ | 3rd Jany, 1866. | ———— | ... | | " |

## Executive Council of Canada, as composed at different periods,

### From 1841 to 1865, inclusive, viz :

#### 13th *February* to 16th *March*, 1841.

Hon. Messrs. Sullivan,      Hon. Messrs. Ogden,
"     Dunn,     "     Draper,
"     Daly,     "     Baldwin,
"     Harrison,     "     Day.

#### 17th *March* to 13th *June*, 1841.

Hon. Messrs. Sullivan,     Hon. Messrs. Draper,
"     Dunn,     "     Baldwin,
"     Daly,     "     Day,
"     Harrison,     "     Killaly.
"     Ogden,

#### 14th *June*, 1841, to 8th *June*, 1842.

Hon. Messrs. Sullivan,     Hon. Messrs. Ogden,
"     Dunn,     "     Draper,
"     Daly,     "     Day.
"     Harrison,     "     Killaly.

## Executive Council of Canada, &c.—(Continued.)

### 9th June to 30th June, 1842.

Hon. Messrs. Sullivan,  
" Dunn,  
" Daly,  
" Harrison,  
" Ogden,  

Hon. Messrs. Draper,  
" Day,  
" Killaly,  
" Hincks.  

### 1st July to 22nd July, 1842.

Hon. Messrs. Sullivan,  
" Dunn,  
" Daly,  
" Harrison,  

Hon. Messrs. Ogden,  
" Draper,  
" Killaly,  
" Hincks.  

### 23rd July to 15th September, 1842.

Hon. Messrs. Sullivan,  
" Dunn,  
" Daly,  
" Harrison,  
" Ogden,  

Hon. Messrs. Draper,  
" Killaly,  
" Hincks,  
" Hy. Sherwood.  

### 16th September to 23rd September, 1842.

Hon. Messrs. LaFontaine,  
" Baldwin,  
" Sullivan,  
" Dunn,  

Hon. Messrs. Daly,  
" Harrison,  
" Killaly,  
" Hincks.  

### 24th September and 25th September, 1842.

Hon. Messrs. LaFontaine,  
" Baldwin,  
" Sullivan,  
" Dunn,  
" Daly,  

Hon. Messrs. Harrison,  
" Killaly,  
" Hincks,  
" Aylwin.  

### 26th September to 12th October, 1842.

Hon. Messrs. Lafontaine,  
" Baldwin,  
" Sullivan,  
" Dunn,  
" Daly,  

Hon. Messrs. Harrison,  
" Killaly,  
" Hincks,  
" Aylwin,  
" Small.  

### 13th October, 1842, to 30th September, 1843.

Hon. Messrs. LaFontaine,  
" Baldwin,  
" Sullivan,  
" Dunn,  
" Daly,  
" Harrison,  

Hon. Messrs. Killaly,  
" Hincks,  
" Aylwin,  
" Small,  
" A. N. Morin.

28th *November* to 11th *December*, **1843.**
Hon. **D. Daly.**

---

12th *December*, 1843, *to* 1st *September*, 1844.
Hon. Messrs. Daly,                    Hon. Mr. Draper.
"         D. B. Viger,

---

2nd *September* to 19th *December*, 1844.
Hon. Messrs. Daly,                Hon. Messrs. Wm. Morris,
"         Viger,                "         D. B. Papineau,
"         Draper,                "         Jas. Smith.

---

20th *December*, 1844, *to* 30th *April*, 1845.
Hon. Messrs. Daly,                Hon. Messrs. Papineau,
"         Viger,                "         Smith,
"         Draper,                "         W. B. Robinson.
"         Morris,

---

1st *May* to 5th *August*, 1845.
Hon. Messrs. Daly,                Hon. Messrs. Morris,
"         Viger,                "         Papineau,
"         Draper,                "         Smith.

---

**6th August**, 1845, *to* 17th *June*, 1846.
**Hon.** Messrs. Daly,                Hon. Messrs. Papineau,
"         Viger,                "         Smith,
"         Draper,                "         Cayley.
"         Morris,

---

**18th June**, 1846, *to* 22nd *April*, 1847.
Hon. Messrs. Daly,                Hon. **Messrs.** Papineau,
"         Draper,                "         Smith,
"         Morris,                "         Cayley.

---

23rd *April* **to** 10th *May*, 1847.
Hon. Messrs. Daly,                Hon. Messrs. Papineau,
"         Draper,                "         Cayley,
"         Morris,                "         Badgley.

---

11th *May* to 21st *May*, 1847.
Hon. Messrs. Daly,                Hon. Messrs. Cayley,
"         Draper,                "         Badgley,
"         Morris,                "         J. A. Macdonald
"         Papineau,

## Executive Council of Canada, &c.—(Continued.)

### 22nd May to 26th May, 1847.

Hon. Messrs. Daly,
" Draper,
" Morris, .
" Papineau,

Hon. Messrs. Cayley,
" Badgley,
" Macdonald,
" J. H. Cameron.

### 29th and 30th May, 1847.

Hon. Messrs. Daly,
" Morris,
" Papineau,
" Cayley,

Hon. Messrs. Badgley,
" Macdonald,
" Cameron,
" Henry Sherwood.

### 31st May to 7th December, 1847.

Hon. Messrs. Daly,
" Morris,
" Papineau,
" Cayley,
" Badgley,

Hon. Messrs. J. A. Macdonald,
" J. H. Cameron,
" H. Sherwood,
" McGill.

### 8th December, 1847, to 10th March, 1848.

Hon. Messrs. Daly,
" Morris,
" Cayley,
" Badgley,
" J. A. Macdonald,

Hon. Messrs. J. H. Cameron,
" H. Sherwood,
" McGill,
" Brunson.

### 10th March, 1848.

Hon. **L. H.** LaFontaine.

### 11th March, to 25th April, 1848.

Hon. Messrs. LaFontaine,
" Baldwin,
" Sullivan,
" Hincks,
" Aylwin,
" Leslie,

Hon. Messrs. Caron,
" Price,
" L. M. Viger,
" Taché,
" M. Cameron.

### 26th April to 14th September, 1848.

Hon. Messrs. LaFontaine,
" Baldwin,
" Sullivan,
" Hincks,
" Leslie,

Hon. Messrs. Caron,
" Price,
" L. M. Viger,
" Taché,
" M. Cameron.

## Executive Council of Canada, &c.—(*Continued.*)

### 15th September, 1848, to 26th November, 1849.

| Hon. Messrs. | LaFontaine, | Hon. Messrs. | Price, |
|---|---|---|---|
| " | Baldwin, | " | L. M. Viger, |
| " | Hincks, | " | Taché, |
| " | Leslie, | " | M. Cameron, |
| " | **Caron,** | " | Merritt. |

### 27th November to 12th December, 1849.

| Hon. Messrs. | LaFontaine, | Hon. Messrs. | Price, |
|---|---|---|---|
| " | Baldwin, | " | Taché, |
| " | Hincks, | " | M. Cameron, |
| " . | Leslie, | " | Merritt. |

### 13th December, 1849, to 1st February, 1850.

| Hon. Messrs. | LaFontaine, | Hon. Messrs. | Taché, |
|---|---|---|---|
| " | Baldwin, | " | M. Cameron, |
| " | Hincks, | " | Merritt, |
| " | Leslie, | " | Chabot. |
| " | Price, | | |

### 2nd February to 31st March, 1850.

| Hon. Messrs. | LaFontaine, | Hon. Messrs. | Price, |
|---|---|---|---|
| " | Baldwin, | " | Taché, |
| " | Hincks, | " | Merritt, |
| " | Leslie, | " | Chabot. |

### 1st April to 16th April, 1850.

| **Hon. Messrs.** | LaFontaine, | Hon. Messrs. | Price, |
|---|---|---|---|
| " | Baldwin, | " | Taché, |
| " | Hincks, | " | Merritt. |
| " | Leslie, | | |

### 17th April, 1850, to 11th February, 1851.

| Hon. Messrs. | LaFontaine, | Hon. Messrs. | Price, |
|---|---|---|---|
| " | Baldwin, | " | Taché, |
| " | Hincks, | " | Merritt, |
| " | Leslie, | " | Bourret. |

### 12th February to 21st February, 1851.

| Hon. Messrs. | LaFontaine, | Hon. Messrs. | Price, |
|---|---|---|---|
| " | Baldwin, | " | Taché, |
| " | Hincks, | " | Bourret. |
| " | Leslie, | | |

### 22nd February to 27th October, 1851.

Hon. Messrs. LaFontaine,  
" Baldwin,  
" Hincks,  
" Leslie,  

Hon. Messrs. Price,  
" Taché,  
" Bourret,  
" Jas. Morris.

---

### 28th October, 1851, to 22nd September, 1852.

Hon. Messrs. Taché,  
" Hincks,  
" J. Morris,  
" A. N. Morin,  
" Caron,  

Hon. Messrs. M. Cameron,  
" Rolph,  
" Drummond,  
" Richards,  
" Young.

---

### 23rd September, 1852, to 21st June, 1853.

Hon. Messrs. Taché,  
" Hincks,  
" J. Morris,  
" A. N. Morin,  
" Caron,  

Hon. Messrs. M. Cameron,  
" Rolph,  
" Drummond,  
" Richards,  
" Chabot.

---

### 22nd June to 14th August, 1853.

Hon. Messrs. Taché,  
" Hincks,  
" J. Morris,  
" A. N. Morin,  
" Caron,  

Hon. Messrs. M. Cameron,  
" Rolph,  
" Drummond,  
" Chabot,  
" Ross.

---

### 15th August to 30th August, 1853.

Hon. Messrs. Taché,  
" Hincks,  
" J. Morris,  
" A. N. Morin,  
" M. Cameron,  

Hon. Messrs. Rolph,  
" Drummond,  
" Chabot,  
" Ross.

---

### 31st August, 1853, to 10th September, 1854.

Hon. Messrs. Taché,  
" Hincks,  
" J. Morris,  
" A. N. Morin,  
" M. Cameron,  

Hon. Messrs. Rolph,  
" Drummond,  
" Chabot,  
" Ross,  
" Chauveau.

---

### 11th September, 1854, to 26th January, 1855.

Hon. Messrs. Taché,  
" J. A. Macdonald,  
" A. N. Morin,  
" Drummond,  
" Chabot,  

Hon. Messrs. Ross,  
" Chauveau,  
" MacNab,  
" Cayley,  
" Spence.

### 27th January, 1855, to 18th April, 1856.

| Hon. Messrs. | Taché, | Hon. Messrs. | Cayley, |
|---|---|---|---|
| " | J. A. Macdonald, | " | Spence, |
| " | Drummond, | " | Cauchon, |
| " | Ross, | " | Lemieux, |
| " | MacNab, | " | **Cartier.** |

### 19th April to 23rd May, 1856.

| Hon. Messrs. | Taché | Hon. Messrs. | Spence, |
|---|---|---|---|
| " | J. A. Macdonald, | " | Cauchon, |
| " | Drummond, | " | Lemieux, |
| " | MacNab, | " | Cartier, |
| " | Cayley, | " | J. C. Morrison. |

### 24th May, 1856, to 30th April, 1857.

| Hon. Messrs. | Taché, | Hon. Messrs. | Lemieux, |
|---|---|---|---|
| " | J. A. Macdonald, | " | Cartier, |
| " | Cayley, | " | Morrison, |
| " | Spence, | " | Terrill, |
| " | Cauchon, | " | Vankoughnet. |

### 1st May to 9th November, 1857.

| Hon. Messrs. | Taché | Hon. Messrs. | Lemieux, |
|---|---|---|---|
| " | J. A. Macdonald, | " | Cartier, |
| " | Cayley, | " | Morrison, |
| " | Spence, | " | Vankoughnet. |

### 10th November to 24th November, 1857.

| Hon. Messrs. | Taché, | Hon. Messrs. | **Lemieux,** |
|---|---|---|---|
| " | J. A. Macdonald, | " | Cartier, |
| " | Cayley, | " | Morrison, |
| " | Spence, | " | Vankoughnet, |

### 25th November, 1857.

| Hon. Messrs. | Taché, | Hon. Messrs. | Cartier, |
|---|---|---|---|
| " | J. A. Macdonald, | " | Morrison, |
| " | Cayley, | " | Vankoughnet, |
| " | Spence, | " | Sicotte. |
| " | Lemieux, | | |

### 26th November 1857 to 1st February, 1858.

| **Hon.** Messrs. | J. A. Macdonald, | Hon. Messrs. | Vankoughnet, |
|---|---|---|---|
| " | Cartier, | " | Sicotte, |
| " | Cayley, | " | Belleau, |
| " | Spence, | " | Alleyn, |
| " | Morrison, | " | Loranger. |

## Executive Council of Canada, &c.—(Continued.)

### 2nd February to 29th July, 1858.

| | |
|---|---|
| Hon. Messrs. J. A. Macdonald, | Hon. Messrs. Belleau, |
| " Cartier, | " Alleyn, |
| " Cayley, | " Loranger, |
| " Vankoughnet, | " Ross, |
| " Sicotte, | " S. Smith. |

### 30th July to 1st August, 1858.

. . . . . . . . . . . . . . . . . . . . . . . . . . . . . . . . . . . . . . . . . . .

### 2nd to 4th August, 1858.

| | |
|---|---|
| Hon. Messrs. Brown, | Hon. Messrs. J. S. Macdonald, |
| " A. A. Dorion, | " Holton, |
| " J. Morris, | " Mowat, |
| " Drummond, | " J. E. Thibaudeau, |
| " Lemieux, | " Foley. |

### 5th August, 1858.

. . . . . . . . . . . . . . . . . . . . . . . . . . . . . . . . . . . . . . . . . . .

### 6th August, 1858.

| | |
|---|---|
| Hon. Messrs. Cartier, | Hon. Messrs. Alleyn, |
| " J. A. Macdonald, | " Sy. Smith. |
| " Vankoughnet, | " Galt, |
| " Sicotte, | " Rose, |
| " Belleau, | " Geo. Sherwood. |

### 7th August to 24th December, 1858.

| | |
|---|---|
| Hon. Messrs. Cartier, | Hon. Messrs. Sy. Smith, |
| " J. A. Macdonald, | " Galt, |
| " Vankoughnet, | " Rose, |
| " Sicotte, | " G. Sherwood, |
| " Belleau, | " J. Ross. |
| " Alleyn, | |

### 25th December, 1858, to 18th January, 1860.

| | |
|---|---|
| Hon. Messrs. Cartier, | Hon. Messrs. Sy. Smith, |
| " J. A. Macdonald, | " Galt, |
| " Vankoughnet, | " Rose, |
| " Belleau, | " G. Sherwood, |
| " Alleyn, | " J. Ross. |

## Executive Council of Canada, &c.—(Continued.)

### 19th January to 21st February, 1860.

Hon. Messrs. Cartier,
" J. A. Macdonald,
" Vankoughnet,
" Belleau,
" Alleyn,
" Sy. Smith,

Hon. Messrs. Galt,
" Rose,
" G. Sherwood,
" J. Ross,
" **L.** S. Morin.

### 22nd February, 1860, to 12th June, 1861.

Hon. Messrs. Cartier,
" J. A. Macdonald,
" Vankoughnet,
" Belleau,
" Alleyn,
" Sy. Smith,

Hon. Messrs. Galt,
" Rose,
" G. Sherwood,
" J. Ross,
" L. S. Morin,
" J. C. Morrison.

### 13th June, 1861, to 18th March, 1862.

Hon. Messrs. Cartier,
" J. A. Macdonald,
" Vankoughnet,
" Belleau,
" Alleyn,
" Sy. Smith,

Hon. Messrs. Galt,
" G. Sherwood,
" J. Ross,
" L. S. Morin,
" J. C. Morrison,
" Cauchon.

### 19th March to 26th March, 1862.

Hon. Messrs. Cartier,
" J. A. Macdonald,
" Belleau,
" Alleyn,
" Sy. Smith,

Hon. Messrs. Galt,
" G. Sherwood,
" J. Ross,
" L. S. Morin,
" Cauchon.

### 27th March to 23rd May, 1862.

Hon. Messrs. Cartier,
" J. A. Macdonald,
" Belleau,
" Alleyn,
" Sy. Smith,
" Galt,

Hon. Messrs. G. Sherwood,
" L. S. Morin,
" Cauchon,
" Patton,
" J. B. Robinson,
" Carling.

### 24th May, 1862, to 27th January, 1863.

**Hon.** Messrs. J. S. Macdonald,
" L. V. Sicotte,
" Jas. Morris,
" A. A. Dorion,
" M. H. Foley,
" McDougall,

Hon. Messrs. Howland,
" Tessier,
" McGee,
" Evanturel,
" **A.** Wilson,
" Abbott,

## Executive Council of Canada, &c.—(Continued.)

### 28th January to 6th March, 1863.

Hon. Messrs. J. S. Macdonald,  
" Sicotte,  
" Jas. Morris,  
" M. H. Foley,  
" McDougall,  
" Howland,  

Hon. Messrs. Tessier,  
" McGee,  
" Evanturel,  
" A. Wilson,  
" Abbott,  
" J. O. Bureau.

### 7th March to 10th May, 1863.

Hon. Messrs. J. S. Macdonald,  
" Sicotte,  
" M. H. Foley,  
" McDougall,  
" Howland,  
" Tessier,  

Hon. Messrs. McGee,  
" Evanturel,  
" A. Wilson,  
" Abbott,  
" Bureau,  
" Ferguson Blair.

### 11th to 15th May, 1863.

Hon. Messrs. J. S. Macdonald,  
" Sicotte,  
" Foley,  
" McDougall,  
" Howland,  
" Tessier,  

Hon. Messrs. McGee,  
" Evanturel,  
" Abbott,  
" Bureau,  
" Ferguson Blair.

### 16th to 27th May, 1863.

Hon. Messrs. J. S. Macdonald,  
" A. A. Dorion,  
" McDougall,  
" Howland,  
" Tessier,  
" Abbott,  

Hon. Messrs. Ferguson Blair,  
" Holton,  
" Mowat,  
" Isid. Thibaudeau,  
" L. Letellier,  
" L. Wallbridge.

### 28th May to 23rd July, 1863.

Hon. Messrs. J. S. Macdonald,  
" Dorion,  
" McDougall,  
" Howland,  
" Holton,  
" Mowat,  

Hon. Messrs. Thibaudeau,  
" Letellier,  
" L. Wallbridge,  
" Drummond,  
" Huntington.

### 24th July to 12th August, 1863.

Hon. Messrs. J. S. Macdonald,  
" A. A. Dorion,  
" McDougall,  
" Howland,  
" Ferguson **Blair,**  
" Holton,  

Hon. Messrs. Mowat,  
" Isid. Thibaudeau,  
" Letellier,  
" L. Wallbridge,  
" Huntington,  
" Laframboise.

3

## Executive Council of Canada, &c.—(*Continued.*)

### 13th *August* to 25th *December*, 1863.

| | | | |
|---|---|---|---|
| Hon. Messrs. | J. S. Macdonald, | Hon. Messrs. | Mowat, |
| " | A. A. Dorion, | " | Isid. Thibaudeau, |
| " | McDougall, | " | Letellier, |
| " | Howland, | " | Huntington, |
| " | Fergusson Blair, | " | Laframboise. |
| " | Holton, | | |

### 26th *December*, 1863, to 30th *January*, 1864.

| | | | |
|---|---|---|---|
| Hon. Messrs. | J. S. Macdonald, | Hon. Messrs. | Mowat, |
| " | A. A. Dorion, | " | Isid. Thibaudeau, |
| " | McDougall, | " | Letellier, |
| " | Howland, | " | Huntington, |
| " | Fergusson Blair, | " | Laframboise, |
| " | Holton, | " | A. N. Richards, |

### 31st *January* to 29th *March*, 1864.

| | | | |
|---|---|---|---|
| Hon. Messrs. | J. S. Macdonald, | Hon. Messrs. | Mowat, |
| " | A. A. Dorion, | " | Isid. Thibaudeau, |
| " | McDougall, | " | Letellier, |
| " | Howland, | " | Huntingdon, |
| " | Fergusson Blair, | " | Laframboise. |
| " | Holton, | | |

### 30th *March* to 29th *June*, 1864.

| | | | |
|---|---|---|---|
| Hon. Messrs. | Sir E. P. Taché, | Hon. Messrs. | McGee, |
| " | J. A. Macdonald, | " | Buchanan, |
| " | Cartier, | " | Chapais, |
| " | Galt, | " | Simpson, |
| " | A. Campbell, | " | H. L. Langevin, |
| " | H. M. Foley, | " | Cockburn. |

### 30th *June* to 19th *November*, 1864.

| | | | |
|---|---|---|---|
| Hon. Messrs. | Sir E. P. Taché, | Hon. Messrs. | Chapais, |
| " | J. A. Macdonald, | " | H. L. Langevin, |
| " | Cartier, | " | Cockburn, |
| " | Galt, | " | Brown, |
| " | Campbell, | " | Mowat, |
| " | McGee, | " | McDougall. |

### 20th to 23rd *November*, 1864.

| | | | |
|---|---|---|---|
| Hon. Messrs. | Sir E. P. Taché, | Hon. Messrs. | Chapais, |
| " | J. A. Macdonald, | " | Langevin, |
| " | Cartier, | " | Cockburn, |
| " | Galt, | " | Brown, |
| " | Campbell, | " | McDougall. |
| " | McGee, | | |

## Executive Council of Canada, &c.—(Continued.)

### 24th November, 1864, to 30th July, 1865.

| | | | |
|---|---|---|---|
| Hon. Messrs. | Sir E. P. Taché, | Hon. Messrs. | Chapais, |
| " | J. A. Macdonald, | " | Langevin, |
| " | Cartier, | " | Cockburn, |
| " | Galt, | " | Brown, |
| " | Campbell, | " | McDougall, |
| " | McGee, | " | Howland. |

### 31st July to 6th August, 1865.

| | | | |
|---|---|---|---|
| Hon. Messrs. | J. A. Macdonald, | Hon. Messrs. | Langevin, |
| " | Cartier, | " | Cockburn, |
| " | Galt, | " | Brown, |
| " | Campbell, | " | McDougall, |
| " | McGee, | " | Howland, |
| " | Chapais, | | |

### 7th August to 21st December, 1865.

| | | | |
|---|---|---|---|
| Hon. Messrs. | Sir N. F. Belleau, | Hon. Messrs. | Chapais, |
| " | J. A. Macdonald, | " | Langevin, |
| " | Cartier, | " | Cockburn, |
| " | Galt, | " | Brown, |
| " | Campbell, | " | McDougall, |
| " | McGee, | " | Howland. |

### 22nd to 31st December, 1865.

| | | | |
|---|---|---|---|
| Hon. Messrs. | Sir N. F. Belleau, | Hon. Messrs. | Chapais, |
| " | J. A. Macdonald, | " | Langevin, |
| " | Cartier, | " | Cockburn, |
| " | Galt, | " | McDougall, |
| " | Campbell, | " | Howland. |
| " | McGee, | | |

Offices held by the Members of the Executive Council of Canada, from
1841 to 1865, inclusive.

| NAMES. | FROM | TO |
|---|---|---|
| ABBOTT, HON. J. J. C. Solicitor General for L. C., and Member of Executive Council. M. P. P., Argenteuil, 6th, 7th, and 8th Parliaments. | 24th May, 1862, | 27th May, 1863. |
| ALLEYN, HON. CHS. Member of Executive Council, Chief Commissioner of Public Works and Member of the Board of Railway Commissioners...................... | 26th November, 1857, | 29th July, 1858. |
| Member of Executive Council and Provincial Secretary..... M. P. P., Quebec City, 5th, 6th, 7th and 8th Parliaments. | 6th August, 1858, | 23rd May, 1862. |
| AYLWIN, HON. T. C. Member of Executive Council and Solicitor General for L. C. | 24th September, 1842, | 27th November, 1843. |
| Member of Executive Council and Solicitor General, L. C... M. P. P., Portneuf, 1st Parlt.... " Quebec, City, 2d and 3rd Parliaments. | 12th March 1848, | 25th April, 1848. |
| BADGLEY, HON. W. Member of Executive Council and Attorney General, L. C.. M. P. P., Missisquoi, 2d, 3rd, and 4th Parliaments. | 23rd April, 1847, | 10th March, 1848. |
| BALDWIN, HON. R. Member of Executive Council and Solicitor General, U. C .. | 13th February, 1841, | 13th June, 1841. |
| Member of Executive Council.. | 16th September, 1842, | 27th November, 1843. |
| Attorney General, U. C........ | 17th September, 1842, | 12th December, 1843. |
| Member of Executive Council and Attorney General, U. C. M. P. P., Hastings, 1st Parlt. " Rimouski, 1st " " York, 4th R., 2nd Parlt. " " N. R., 3rd " | 11th March, 1848, | 27th October, 1851. |

Offices held by the Members of the Executive Council, &c.—(Continued.)

| NAMES. | FROM | TO |
|---|---|---|
| BELLEAU, SIR N. F. Member of the Leg. Council ... | 22nd October, 1852, | |
| Speaker of the Legislative Council and Member of the Executive Council .............. | 26th November, 1857, | 29th July, 1858. |
| " " .. | 6th August, 1858 | 22nd May, 1862. |
| Speaker of Legislative Council. | 7th August, 1858, | 19th March, 1862. |
| Member of Executive Council (Premier) and Recr. General. | 7th August, 1865, | |
| | | |
| BLAIR, HON. A. J. F. (1) Member of Executive Council.. | 7th March, 1863, | 29th March, 1864. |
| Receiver General............. | 7th March, 1863. | 13th May, 1863. |
| Provincial Secretary .......... | 16th May, 1863, | 29th March, 1864. |
| | | |
| BOURRET, HON. JOS. Member of Legislative Council. | 21st November, 1848, | 9th March, 1852. |
| Member and President of Executive Council .............. | 17th April, 1850, | 27th October, 1851. |
| Assist. Com. of Public Works .. | 17th April, 1850, | 11th February, 1851. |
| Chief " " .. | 12th February, 1851, | 27th October, 1851. |
| Member of Board of Railway Commissioners ............. | 30th August, 1851, | 27th October, 1851. |
| | | |
| BROWN, HON. GEO. Member of Executive Council, Inspector General, and Member of Board of Railway Comrs ... | 2nd August, 1858, | 8th August, 1858. |
| Member and President of the Executive Council.......... | 30th June, 1864, | 21st December, 1865. |
| M. P. P., Kent, 4th Parliament. Do. Lambton, 5th do. . Do. N. R. Oxford and Toronto City, 6th Parliament. M. P. P., S. R. Oxford, 7th and 8th Parliament. | | |
| | | |
| BRUNEAU, HON. F. P. Member of Legislative Council. | 9th June, 1841, | 4th March, 1851. |
| Member of the Executive Council and Receiver General .... | 8th December, 1847, | 10th March, 1848. |
| | | |
| BUCHANAN, HON. ISAAC. Member and President of the Executive Council .......... | 30th March, 1864, | 29th June, 1864. |

(1). Mr. Blair was further appointed Member and President of the Executive Council, on 3rd January, 1866.

**Offices held by the Members of the Executive Council, &c.—(*Continued.*)**

| NAMES. | FROM | TO |
|---|---|---|
| M. P. P., Toronto City, 1st Parlt. Do. Hamilton City, 6th, 7th and 8th Parliaments. | | |
| BUREAU, HON. J. O. Member of the Executive Council and Provincial Secretary.. | 28th January, 1863.. | 15th May, 1863. |
| Member of Legislative Assembly for Napierville, 5th, 6th and 7th Parliaments. Member of Legislative Council for DeLorimier, elected in 1862. | | |
| CAMERON, HON. J. H. Solicitor General, U. C......... | 1st July, 1846...... | 10th March, 1848. |
| Member of Executive Council.. | 22nd May, 1847..... | 10th March, 1848. |
| Member of Legislative Assembly for Town of Cornwall, 2nd and 3rd Parlts., City of Toronto, 5th Parlt., Peel 7th and 8th Parliaments. | | |
| CAMERON, HON. M. Member of Executive Council and Asst. Com. of Pub. Works. | 11th March, 1848 ... | 1st February, 1850. |
| Member of Executive Council.. | 28th October, 1851 .. | 10th September, 1854. |
| President of " .. | 28th October, 1851 .. | 16th August, 1853. |
| Minister of Agriculture........ | 10th November, 1852. | 16th August, 1853, |
| Postmaster General and Member of Board of Railway Comrs... | 17th August, 1853... | 10th September, 1854. |
| Government Director of Grand Trunk Railway............. | 11th November, 1852. | 10th September, 1854. |
| Member of Legislative Assembly for Lanark, 1st and 2nd Parlts., Kent, 3rd Parlt., Huron, 4th Parlt., Lambton, 6th Parlt., Member of Legislative Council for St. Clair, elected in 1860 . | | |
| CAMPBELL, HON. A. Member of Executive Council and Commissioner of Crown Lands.................... | 30th March, 1864, | ——————— |
| Member of Legislative Council for Cataraque, elected in 1858. | | |
| CARLING, HON. J. Member of Executive Council and Receiver General....... | 27th **March,** 1862, | 23rd May, 1862. |

Offices held by the Members of the Executive Council, &c.—(*Continued.*)

| NAMES. | FROM | TO |
|---|---|---|
| Member of Legislative Assembly for City of London, 6th, 7th and 8th Parliaments. | | |
| | | |
| CARON, HON. R. E. | | |
| Member of Legislative Council. | 9th June, 1841, | 16th March, 1857. |
| Speaker of " " .. | 8th November, 1843, | 19th May, 1847. |
| " " " .. | 11th March, 1848, | 14th August, 1853. |
| Member of Executive Council.. | 11th March, 1848, | 26th November, 1849. |
| " " " .. | 28th October, 1851, | 14th August, 1852. |
| Government Director of Grand Trunk Railway?.............. | 20th November, 1852, | 14th August, 1853. |
| | | |
| CARTIER, HON. G. E. | | |
| Member of Executive Council.. | 27th January, 1855, | 29th July, 1856. |
| Provincial Secretary.......... | 27th January, 1855, | 23rd May, 1856. |
| Attorney General, L. C........ | 24th May, 1856, | 29th July, 1858. |
| Member of Executive Council.. | 6th August, 1856, | 23rd May, 1862. |
| Inspector General............. | 6th August, 1858, | 6th August, 1858. |
| Attorney General, L. C........ | 7th August, 1858, | 23rd May, 1862. |
| Member of Executive Council and Attorney General, L. Ca.. | 30th March, 1864, | ———— |
| Government Director of Grand Trunk Railway (West)...... | 11th November, 1852, | 10th May, 1853. |
| Member of Legislative Assembly for Verchères, 3rd, 4th, 5th and 6th Parliaments; Montreal City, (East,) 7th and 8th Parliaments. | | |
| | | |
| CAUCHON, HON. J. | | |
| Member of Executive Council and Commissioner of Crown Lands................ ........ | 27th January, 1855, | 30th April, 1857. |
| Member of Executive Council and Commissioner of Public Works........ ............. | 13th June, 1861, | 23rd May, 1862. |
| Member of Legislative Assembly for Montmorenci, 2nd, 3rd, 4th, 5th, 6th, 7th and 8th Parliaments. | | |
| | | |
| CAYLEY, HON. W. | | |
| Member of Executive Council and Inspector General....... | 6th August, 1845, | 10th March, 1848. |

Offices held by the Members of the Executive Council, &c.—(*Continued.*)

| NAMES. | FROM | TO |
|---|---|---|
| Member of Executive Council, Inspector General, and member of Board of Railway Commissioners.................... | 11th September, 1854, | 29th July, 1858. |
| Government Director of Grand Trunk R. R................ | 3rd November, 1854, | 28th July, 1857. |
| Member of Legislative Assembly for Huron, 2nd, and 3rd Parliaments, Huron and Bruce 5th Parliament, Renfrew 6th Parliament. | | |
| CHABOT, HON. J. | | |
| Member of Executive Council and Chief Commissioner of Public Works............. | 13th December, 1849, | 31st March, 1850. |
| Members of Executive Council, Chief Commissioner of Public Works, and Member of Board of Railway Commissioners... | 23rd September, 1852, | 26th January, 1855. |
| Government Director of Grand Trunk R. R................ | 20th November, 1852, | 26th January, 1855. |
| Member of Legislative Assembly for Quebec City 1st, 2nd, 3rd, and 5th Parliaments; Bellechasse 4th & 5th Parliaments. | | |
| CHAPAIS, HON. J. C. | | |
| Member of Executive Council and Commissioner of Public Works | 30th March, 1864, | |
| Member of the Legislative Assembly for Kamouraska, 4th, 5th, 6th, 7th, & 8th Parliaments | | |
| CHAUVEAU, HON. P. J. O. | | |
| Solicitor General, L. C......... | 12th November, 1851, | 30th August, 1853. |
| Member of Executive Council and Provincial Secretary..... | **31st** August, 1853, | 26th January, 1855. |
| Member of Legislative Assembly Quebec County, 2nd, 3rd, 4th and 5th Parliaments. | | |
| COCKBURN, HON. J. | | |
| Member of Executive Council and Solicitor General, U. C.. | 30th March, 1864, | |
| Member of Legislative Assembly for Northumberland (W. R.) 7th and 8th Parliaments. | | |

Offices held by the Members of the Executive Council, &c.—(Continued.)

| NAMES. | FROM | TO |
|---|---|---|
| DALY, HON. D. | | |
| Member of Executive Council.. | 13th February, 1841, | 10th March, 1848. |
| Provincial Secretary, L. C..... | 10th February, 1841, | 31st December, 1843. |
| "            Canada. | 1st January, 1844, | 10th March, 1848. |
| Member of the Board of Works. | 21st December, 1841, | 8th June, 1846. |
| Member of Legislative Assembly for Megantic 1st, 2nd, and 3rd Parliaments. | | |
| | | |
| DAY, HON. C. D. | | |
| Member of Executive Council and Solicitor General L. C... | 13th February, 1841. | 20th June, 1842. |
| Member of Legislative Assembly for County of Ottawa, 1st Parliament. | | |
| | | |
| DORION, HON. A. A. | | |
| Member of Executive Council and Commissioner of Crown Lands..................... | 2nd August 1858, | 4th August, 1858. |
| Member of Executive Council and Provincial Secretary..... | 24th May, 1862, | 27th January, 1863. |
| Member of Executive Council and Attorney General, L. C.. | 16th May, 1863. | 29th March, 1864. |
| Member of Legislative Assembly for Montreal City, 5th and 6th Parliaments. | | |
| Hochelaga, 7th and 8th Parliaments. | | |
| | | |
| DRAPER, HON. W. H. | | |
| Member of Executive Council and Attorney General, U. C.. | 13th February, 1841, | 15th September, 1842. |
| Member of Executive Council.. | 12th December, 1843, | 28th May, 1847. |
| Attorney General, U. C........ | 1st September, 1844, | 28th May, 1847. |
| Member of the Board of Works. | 4th October, 1844, | 8th June, 1846. |
| Member of Legislative Assembly for Russell, 1st Parliament; Town of London, 2nd Parlt. ; of Legislative Council, from 10th April, 1843, to 30th January, 1845. | | |
| | | |
| DRUMMOND, HON. L. T. | | |
| Solicitor General, L. C......... | 7th June, 1848, | 27th October, 1851. |
| Member of Executive Council and Attorney General, L. C.. | 28th October, 1851, | 23rd May, 1856. |

**Offices held by the Members of the Executive Council, &c.—(*Continued.*)**

| NAMES. | FROM | TO |
|---|---|---|
| Member of Executive Council and Attorney General, L. C.. | 2nd August, 1858, | 4th August, 1858. |
| Member of Executive Council and Comr. of Public Works.. | 28th May, 1863, | 23rd July, 1863. |
| Government Director of Grand Trunk Railway............. | 20th November, 1852, | 23rd May, 1856. |
| Member of Legislative Assembly for Portneuf, 2nd Parliament; Shefford, 3rd, 4th, 5th, and 6th Parliament; Lotbinière, 6th Parlt.; and Rouville, 7th Parlt. | | |
| | | |
| DUNN, HON. J. H. | | |
| Member of Executive Council.. | 13th February, 1841, | 27th November, 1843. |
| Receiver General............. | 10th February, 1841, | 31st December, 1843. |
| Member of Legislative Assembly for Toronto City, 1st. Parlt. | | |
| | | |
| EVANTUREL, HON. F. | | |
| Member of Executive Council and Minister of Agriculture.. | 24th May, 1862, | 15th May, 1863. |
| Member of Legislative Assembly for Quebec County, 5th, 7th and 8th Parliaments. | | |
| | | |
| FOLEY, HON. M. H. | | |
| Member of Executive Council, Postmaster General and Member of the Board of Railway Commissioners............. | 2nd August, 1858, | 4th August, 1858. |
| Member of Executive Council and Postmaster General...... | 24th May, 1862, | 15th May, 1863. |
| Member of Executive Council and Postmaster General..... | 30th March, 1864, | 29th June, 1864. |
| Member of Legislative Assembly for Waterloo, N. R., 5th, 6th, 7th and 8th Parliaments; Perth 7th Parliament. | | |
| | | |
| GALT, HON. A. T. | | |
| Member of Executive Council, Inspector General, and Member of the Board of Railway Commissioners. ............ | 6th August, 1858, | 23rd May, 1862. |
| Member of Executive Council and Minister of Finance..... | 30th March, 1864, | |
| Government Director of Grand Trunk Railway............. | 11th November, 1852, | 28th July, 1857. |

Offices held by the Members of the Executive Council, &c.—(Continued.)

| NAMES. | FROM | TO |
|---|---|---|
| Member of the Legislative Assembly for Sherbrooke, County, 3rd Parliament; Town of Sherbrooke, 4th, 5th, 6th, 7th and 8th Parliaments. | | |
| HARRISON, HON. S. B. Member of Executive Council and Provincial Secretary, U. C. | 13th February, 1841, | 30th September, 1843. |
| Member of the Board of Works. | 21st December, 1841, | 3rd October, 1844. |
| Member of Legislative Assembly for Kingston, 1st Parliament; Kent, 2nd Parliament. | | |
| HINCKS, HON. F. Member of Executive Council and Inspector General....... | 9th June, 1842, | 27th November, 1843. |
| Member of Executive Council and Inspector General....... | 11th March, 1848, | 10th September, 1854. |
| Member of the Board of Railway Commissioners............. | 30th August, 1851, | 10th September, 1854. |
| Government Director of Grand Trunk Railway............. | 11th November, 1852, | 10th September, 1854. |
| Member of Legislative Assembly for Oxford, 1st, 3rd and 4th Parlts., Niagara Town, 4th Parlt., Oxford, S. R., 5th Parlt., and Renfrew, 5th Parliament. | | |
| HOLTON, HON. L. H. Member of Executive Council, Chief Comr. of Public Works, and Member of the Board of Railway Commissioners..... | 2nd August, 1858, | 4th August, 1858. |
| Member of Executive Council and Minister of Finance..... | 16th May, 1863, | 29th March, 1864. |
| Government Director of Grand Trunk Railway......... | 11th November, 1852, | 28th July, 1857. |
| Member of Legislative Assembly, for Montreal City, 5th Parlt., Chateauguai, 8th Parlt., of Legislative Council, for Victoria, elected in 1862 | | |
| HOWLAND, HON. W. P. Member of Executive Council.. | 24th May, 1862, | 29th March, 1864. |
| Inspector General ............ | 24th May, 1862, | 15th May, 1863. |
| Receiver General............ | 16th May, 1863, | 29th March, 1864. |

| NAMES. | FROM | TO |
|---|---|---|
| Member of Executive Council and Postmaster General ..... Member of Legislative Assembly for W. R. of York, 6th, 7th and 8th Parliaments. | 24th November, 1864, | |
| HUNTINGTON, HON. L. S. Member of Executive Council and Solicitor General, L. C .. Member of Legislative Assembly, for Shefford, 7th and 8th Parlts. | 28th May, 1863, | 29th March, 1864. |
| KILLALY, HON. H. H. Member of Executive Council.. Chairman of the Board of Works. Asst. Comr. of Public Works ... Member of Board of Railway Commissioners ............. Member of Legislative Assembly for the Town of London, 1st Parliament. | 17th March, 1841, 21st December, 1841, 12th February, 1851, 30th August, 1851, | 27th November, 1843 8th June, 1846. 6th May, 1859. 6th May, 1859. |
| LAFONTAINE, SIR L. H. Member of Executive Council and Attorney General, L. C .. Member of Executive Council and Attorney General, L. C .. Member of Legislative Assembly for 4th Riding of York, 1st Parlt., Terrebonne, 2nd and 3rd Parlts., Montreal City, 3rd Parliament. | 16th September, 1842. 10th March, 1848, | 27th November, 1843 27th October, 1851. |
| LAFRAMBOISE, HON. M. Member of Executive Council and Comr. of Public Works .. Member of Legislative Assembly for Bagot, 6th, 7th and 8th Parliaments. | 24th July, 1863, | 23th March, 1864. |
| LANGEVIN, HON. H. L. Member of Executive Council and Solicitor General, L. C .. Member of the Legislative Assembly for Dorchester, 6th, 7th and 8th Parliaments. | 30th March, 1864, | |

| NAMES. | FROM | TO |
|---|---|---|
| **LEMIEUX, HON. F.**<br>Member of Executive Council, Chief Comr. of Public Works, and Member of Board of Railway Commissioners.......... | 27th January, 1855, | 25th November, 1857. |
| Member of Executive Council, Receiver General and Member of the Board of Railway Coms. | 2nd August, 1858, | 4th August, 1858 |
| Government Director of Grand Trunk R. R................ | 20th November, 1852, | 19th November, 1853. |
| Member of Legislative Assembly for Dorchester, 2nd, 3rd and 4th Parlts., Levis, 5th and 6th Parlts., of the Legislative Council, for De la Durantaye, elected in 1862. | | |
| **LESLIE, HON. J.**<br>Member of Executive Council.. | 11th March, 1848, | 27th October, 1851. |
| President of " " .. | 11th March, 1848, | 14th September, 1848. |
| Provincial Secretary.......... | 15th September, 1848, | 27th October, 1851. |
| Member of the Legislative Assembly for Verchères, 1st, 2d and 3rd Parliaments—Member of the Legislative Council from | 23rd May, 1848. | |
| **LETELLIER DE ST. JUST, HON. L.**<br>Member of Executive Council and Minister of Agriculture... | 16th May, 1863, | 29th March, 1864. |
| Member of Legislative Assembly for Kamouraska, 3rd Parlt.... | | |
| Member of Legislative Council for Grandville, elected in 1860. | | |
| **LORANGER, HON. T. J. J.**<br>Member of Executive Council and Provincial Secretary..... | 26th November, 1857 | 29th July, 1858. |
| Member of the Legislative Assembly for Laprairie, 5th, 6th and 7th Parliaments. | | |
| **MACDONALD, HON. J. A.**<br>Member of Executive Council.. | 11th May, 1847, | 10th March, 1848. |
| Receiver General............ | 21st May, 1847, | 7th December, 1847. |
| Commissioner of Crown Lands.. | 8th December, 1847, | 10th March, 1848. |
| Member of Executive Council and Attorney General, U. C.. | 11th September, 1854, | 28th July, 1858. |

| NAMES. | FROM | TO |
|---|---|---|
| Member of Executive Council.. | 6th August, 1858, | 23rd May, 1862. |
| Postmaster General............ | 6th August, 1858, | 7th August, 1858. |
| Attorney General, U. C........ | 7th August, 1858, | 23rd May, 1862. |
| Member of Executive Council and Attorney General, U. C.. | 30th March, 1864, | |
| Member of Legislative Assembly for City of Kingston, 2d, 3d, 4th, 5th, 6th, 7th and 8th Parliaments. | | * |
| MACDONALD, HON. J. S. | | |
| Solicitor General, U. C........ | 14th December, 1849, | 11th November, 1851. |
| Speaker of Legislative Assembly. | 19th August, 1852, | 23rd June, 1854. |
| Member of Executive Council and Attorney General, U. C.. | 2nd August, 1858, | 4th August, 1858. |
| Member of Executive Council and Attorney General, U. C.. | 24th May, 1862, | 29th March, 1864. |
| Member of Legislative Assembly for Glengarry, 1st, 2d, 3d, 4th and 5th Parlts.—Town of Cornwall, 6th, 7th and 8th Parlts.. | | |
| McDOUGALL, HON. W. | | |
| Member of Executive Council and Commissioner of Crown Lands.................... | 24th May, 1862, | 29th March, 1864. |
| Member of Executive Council and Provincial Secretary.... | 30th June, 1864, | ——— |
| Member of Legislative Assembly for N. R. of Oxford, 1st and 7th Parlts.—N. R. of Ontario, 8th Parlt.—N. R. of Lanark, 8th Parliament. | | |
| McGEE, HON. T. D. | | |
| Member and President of the Executive Council.......... | 24th May, 1862, | 15th May, 1863. |
| Member of Executive Council and Minister of Agriculture.. | 30th March, 1864, | |
| Member of Legislative Assembly for Montreal City, 6th, 7th and 8th Parliaments. | | |
| McGILL, HON. P. | | |
| Member of Legislative Council. | 9th June, 1841, | Died in 1860. |
| Speaker of the Legislative Council...................... | 21st May, 1847, | 10th March, 1848. |
| Member of Executive Council.. | 31st May, 1847, | 10th March, 1848. |

**Offices held by the Members of the Executive Council, &c.—(Continued.)**

| NAMES. | FROM | TO |
|---|---|---|
| **MACNAB, SIR A. N.** | | |
| Speaker of Legislative Assembly | 28th November, 1844, | 24th February, 1848. |
| Adjutant General of Militia..... | 30th June, 1846, | 20th June, 1846. |
| Member and President of the Executive Council and Minister of Agriculture........... | 11th September, 1854, | 24rd May, 1856. |
| Government Director of Grand Trunk Railway............. | 3rd November, 1854, | 28th July, 1857. |
| Member of Legislative Assembly for City of Hamilton, 1st, 2d, 3d, 4th and 5th Parlts.—of Legislative Council, for Western Division, elected in 1860. | | |
| | | |
| **MERRITT, HON. W. H.** | | |
| Member of Executive Council,.. | 15th September, 1848, | 11th February, 1851. |
| President of " " .. | 15th September, 1848, | 7th April, 1850. |
| Chief Commissioner of Public Works .................... | 8th April, 1850, | 11th February, 1851. |
| Member of Legislative Assembly for Lincoln, 1st, 2nd, 3rd, 4th, 5th and 6th Parliaments; of Legislative Council for Niagara Division, elected in 1860. | | |
| | | |
| **MORIN, HON. A. N.** | | |
| Member of Executive Council and Commissioner of Crown Lands..................... | 13th October, 1842, | 27th November, 1843. |
| Speaker of Legislative Assembly, | 25th February, 1848, | 27th October, 1851. |
| Member of Executive Council, | 28th October, 1851, | 26th January, 1855. |
| Provincial Secretary,.......... | 28th October, 1851, | 30th August, 1853. |
| Commissioner of Crown Lands, | 31st August, 1853, | 26th January, 1855. |
| Member of the Legislative Assembly for Nicolet, 1st Parlt.; Saguenay, 1st and 2nd Parliaments; Bellechasse, 2nd and 3rd Parlts.; Terrebonne, 4th Parlt.; Chicoutimi and Tadoussac, 5th Parlt. | | |
| | | |
| **MORIN, HON. L. S.** | | |
| Member of Executive Council and Solicitor General, L. C... | 19th January, 1860, | 23rd May, 1862. |
| Member of Legislative Assembly for Terrebonne, 5th and 6th Parlts.; for Laval, 7th Parliament. | | |

| NAMES. | FROM | TO |
|---|---|---|
| MORRIS, HON. W. | | |
| Member of Legislative Council, | 9th June, 1841, | 29th June, 1858. |
| Member of Executive Council, | 2nd September, 1844, | 10th March, 1848. |
| Receiver General, ............. | 2nd September, 1844, | 20th May, 1847. |
| President of the Executive Council, ........................ | 22nd May, 1847, | 10th March, 1848. |
| Member of the Board of Works, | 4th October, 1844, | 8th June, 1846. |
| | | |
| MORRIS, HON. JAS. | | |
| Member of Legislative Council, | 27th November, 1844, | Died 29th Sept., 1865. |
| Member of the Executive Council, ..................... | 22nd February, 1851, | 10th September, 1854. |
| Postmaster General, ........... | 22nd February, 1851, | 16th August, 1853. |
| Speaker of Legislative Council, | 17th August, 1853, | 10th September, 1854. |
| Member of Executive Council and Speaker of Legislative Council ................ | 2nd August, 1858, | 4th August, 1858. |
| Member of Executive Council and Receiver General ....... | 24th May, 1862, | 6th March, 1863. |
| Member of the Board of Railway Commissioners ............. | 30th August, 1851, | 16th August, 1853. |
| Government Director of Grand Trunk Railway............. | 11th November, 1852, | 10th September, 1854. |
| Member of Legislative Assembly for Leeds, 1st Parliament. | | |
| | | |
| MORRISON, HON. J. C. | | |
| Solicitor General, U. C........ | 22nd June, 1853 .... | 10th September, 1854. |
| Member of Executive Council, Receiver General and Member of Board of Railway Comrs.. | 24th May, 1856, | 2nd February, 1858. |
| Member of Executive Council and Solicitor General, U. C.. | 22nd February, 1860, | 17th March, 1862. |
| Member of the Legislative Assembly for W. R. of York, 3rd Parlt., for Town of Niagara, 4th and 5th Parliaments. | | |
| | | |
| MOWAT, HON. O. | | |
| Member of Executive Council and Provincial Secretary .... | 2nd August, 1858, | 4th August, 1858. |
| Member of Executive Council and Postmaster General ..... | 16th May, 1863, | 29th March, 1864. |
| Member of Executive Council and Postmaster General ..... | 30th June, 1864, | 19th November, 1864. |
| Member of the Legislative Assembly for S. R. of Ontario, 6th, 7th and 8th Parliaments. | | |

Offices held by the Members of the Executive Council, &c.—(Continued.)

| NAMES. | FROM | TO |
|---|---|---|
| OGDEN, HON. C. R. Member of Executive Council and Attorney General, L. C.. Member of the Legislative Assembly, for Town of Three Rivers, 1st Parliament. | 13th February, 1841, | 15th September, 1842. |
| PAPINEAU, HON. D. B. Member of Executive Council and Comr. of Crown Lands .. Member of the Board of Works. Member of the Legislative Assembly for County of Ottawa, 1st and 2nd Parliaments. | 2nd September, 1844, 4th October, 1844, | 7th December, 1847. 8th June, 1846. |
| PATTON, HON. J. Member of Executive Council and Solicitor General, U. C.. Member of Legislative Council for Saugeen Division, elected in 1856. | 27th March, 1862, | 23rd May, 1862. |
| PRICE, HON. J. H. Member of the Executive Council and Comr. of Crown Lands. Member of the Legislative Assembly for 1st R. of York, 1st and 2nd Parliaments; S. R. of York, 3rd Parliament. | 11th March, 1848, | 27th October, 1851. |
| RICHARDS, HON. W. B. Member of Executive Council and Attorney General, U. C.. Member of the Legislative Assembly for Leeds, 3rd and 4th Parliaments. | 28th October, 1851, | 21st June, 1853. |
| RICHARDS, HON. A. N. Member of the Executive Council and Solicitor General, U. C. Member of the Legislative Assembly for S. R. of Leeds, 8th Parliament. | 26th December, 1853, | 30th January, 1854. |
| ROBINSON, HON. W. B. Member of Executive Council and Inspector General....... Chief Comr. of Public Works .. | 20th December, 1844, 22nd June, 1846, | 30th April, 1845. 10th March, 1848. |

4

**Offices held by the Members of the Executive Council, &c.—(*Continued.*)**

| NAMES. | FROM | TO |
|---|---|---|
| Member of Legislative Assembly for Simcoe, 2nd, 3rd, 4th and 5th Parliaments. | | |
| ROBINSON, HON. J. B. Member and President of the Executive Council.......... | 27th March, 1862, | 23rd May, 1862. |
| Member of the Legislative Assembly, for City of Toronto, 6th and 7th Parliaments. | | |
| ROLPH, HON. J. Member of Executive Council.. | 28th October, 1851, | 10th September, 1854. |
| Commissioner of Crown Lands . | 28th October, 1851, | 30th August, 1853. |
| President of the Executive Council and Minister of Agriculture. | 17th August, 1853, | 10th September, 1854. |
| Member of the Legislative Assembly for Norfolk, 4th and 5th Parliaments. | | |
| ROSE, HON. J. Solicitor General, L. C......... | 26th November, 1857, | 1st August, 1858. |
| Member of Executive Council, | 6th August, 1858, | 12th June, 1861. |
| Receiver General, ............ | 6th August, 1858, | 6th August, 1858. |
| Solicitor General, L. C......... | 7th August, 1858, | 10th January, 1859. |
| Chief Commissioner of Public Works,.................... | 11th January, 1859, | 12th June, 1861. |
| Member of the Legislative Assembly for Montreal City, 6th, 7th and 8th Parliaments. | | |
| ROSS, HON. J. Solicitor General, U. C........ | 12th November, 1851, | 21st June, 1853. |
| Member of Executive Council. | 22nd June, 1853, | 18th April, 1856. |
| Attorney General, U. C......... | 22nd June, 1853, | 10th September, 1854. |
| Speaker of Legislative Council. | 11th September, 1854, | 18th April, 1856. |
| Member of Executive Council, Receiver General and Member of the Board of Railway Commissioners ............ | 2nd February, 1858, | 29th July, 1858. |
| Member and President of the Executive Council and Minister of Agriculture...... | 7th August, 1858, | 26th March, 1862. |
| Member of Legislative Council.. | 1st December, 1848, | ———————— |
| Government Director of Grand Trunk Railway............. | 11th November, 1852, | 28th July, 1857. |
| SHERWOOD, HON. H. Member of the Executive Council and Solicitor General, U. C. | 23rd July, 1842, | 15th September, 1842. |

**Offices held by the Members of the Executive Council, &c.—(Continued.)**

| NAMES. | FROM | TO |
|---|---|---|
| Solicitor General, U. C. ....... | 7th October, 1844, | 30th June, 1846. |
| Member of Executive Council and Attorney General,....... | 29th May, 1847, | 10th March, 1848. |
| Member of Legislative Assembly for Toronto City, 1st, 2nd, 3rd and 4th Parliaments. | | |
| | | |
| SHERWOOD, HON. G. | | |
| Member of Executive Council.. | 6th August, 1858, | 23rd May, 1862. |
| Receiver General............. | 7th August, 1858, | 26th March, 1862. |
| Commissioner of Crown Lands. | 27th March, 1862, | 23rd May, 1862. |
| Member of Legislative Assembly for town of Brockville, 1st, 2nd, 3rd, 6th and 7th Parliaments. | | |
| | | |
| SICOTTE, HON. L. V. | | |
| Member of Executive Council and Commissioner of Crown Lands....................... | 17th August, 1853, | 26th August, 1854. |
| Speaker of Legislative Assembly. | 5th September, 1854, | 25th November, 1857. |
| Member of Executive Council and Commissioner of Crown Lands..................... | 25th November, 1857, | 29th July, 1858. |
| Member of Executive Council, Chief Commissioner of Public Works and Member of Board of Railway Commissioners... | 6th August, 1858, | 24th December, 1858. |
| Member of Executive Council and Attorney General, L. C.. | 24th May, 1862, | 15th May, 1863. |
| Member of the Legislative Assembly for St. Hyacinthe, 4th, 5th, 6th, 7th and 8th Parlts. | | |
| | | |
| SIMPSON, HON. J. | | |
| Member of Executive Council and Provincial Secretary..... | 30th March, 1864, | 29th June, 1864. |
| Member of Legislative Assembly for Town of Niagara, 6th, 7th and 8th Parliaments. | | |
| | | |
| SMALL, HON. J. E. | | |
| Member of Executive Council, and Solicitor General, U. C... | 26th September, 1842, | 27th November, 1843. |
| Member of Legislative Assembly for 3rd R. of York, 1st and 2nd Parliaments. | | |

4 *

Offices held by the Members of the Executive Council, &c.—(*Continued.*)

| NAMES. | FROM | TO |
|---|---|---|
| SMITH, HON. JAS.<br>Member of Executive Council, and Attorney General, L. C.. | 2nd September, 1844, | 22nd April, 1847. |
| Member of the Legislative Assembly for Missisquoi, 2nd Parliament. | | |
| SMITH, HON. SIDNEY.<br>Member of Executive Council, Postmaster General, and Member of the Board of Railway Commissioners.............. | 2nd February, 1858, | 29th July, 1858. |
| Member of Executive Council.. | 6th August, 1858, | 23rd May, 1862. |
| President of Executive Council and Minister of Agriculture.. | 6th August, 1858, | 6th August, 1858. |
| Postmaster General and Member of the Board of Railway Commissioners.............. | 7th August, 1858, | 23rd May, 1862. |
| Member of the Legislative Assembly for W. R. of Northumberland, 5th and 6th Parlts.—of Legislative Council, for the Trent Division, elected in 1861, resigned in 1863. | | |
| SPENCE, HON. R.<br>Member of the Executive Council, Postmaster General, and Member of the Board of Railway Commissioners......... | 11th September, 1854, | 1st February, 1858. |
| Member of the Legislative Assembly, for N. R. of Wentworth, 5th Parliament. | | |
| SULLIVAN, HON. R. B.<br>Member and President of the Executive Council......... | 13th February, 1841, | 27th November, 1843. |
| Commissioner of Crown Lands.. | 10th February, 1841, | 30th June, 1841. |
| Member of the Executive Council and Provincial Secretary.. | 11th March, 1848, | 14th September, 1848. |
| Member of the Legislative Council......................... | 9th June, 1841, | 30th May, 1851. |
| TACHÉ, SIR E. P.<br>Deputy Adjutant Genl. of Militia | 1st July, 1846, | 10th March, 1848. |
| Member of the Executive Council........................ | 11th March, 1848, | 25th November, 1857. |

## Offices held by the Members of the Executive Council, &c.—(Continued.)

| NAMES. | FROM | TO |
|---|---|---|
| Chief Commr. of Public Works. | 11th March, 1848, | 8th November, 1849. |
| Receiver General............ | 27th November, 1849, | 23rd May, 1856, |
| Commissioner of Crown Lands.. | 16th July, 1857, | 25th November, 1857 |
| Member of the Executive Council and Receiver General.... | 30th March, 1864, | 30th July, 1865. |
| Member of the Legislative Council.................... | 23rd May, 1848, | 30th July, 1865. |
| Speaker of the Legislative Council.................... | 19th April, 1856, | 25th November, 1857. |
| Member of the Board of Railway Commissioners......... | 30th August, 1851, | 23rd May, 1856. |
| Government Director of the Grand Trunk Railway,...... | 20th November, 1852, | 28th July, 1857. |
| Member of the Legislative Assembly for L'Islet, 1st and 2nd Parliaments. | | |
| | | |
| TERRILL, HON. T. L. | | |
| Member of Executive Council.. | 24th May, 1856, | 9th November, 1857. |
| Provincial Secretary......... | 24th May, 1856, | 25th November, 1857. |
| Members of the Legislative Assembly for Stanstead, 4th, 5th, and 6th Parliaments. | | |
| | | |
| TESSIER, HON. J. U. | | |
| Member of the Executive Council and Commissioner of Public Works.................... | 24th May, 1862, | 27th May, 1863. |
| Member of the Legislative Assembly for Portneuf, 4th Parlt.. | | |
| Member of the Legislative Council for the Gulf Division; elected in 1858. | | |
| | | |
| THIBAUDEAU, HON. J. E. | | |
| Member and President of the Executive Council, and Minister of Agriculture.......... | 2nd August, 1858, | 4th August, 1858. |
| Member of the Legislative Assembly for Portneuf, 5th and 6th Parliaments. | | |
| | | |
| THIBAUDEAU, HON. ISID. | | |
| Member and President of the Executive Council.......... | 16th May, 1863, | 29th March, 1864. |
| Member of the Legislative Assembly for Quebec City, Centre, 8th Parliament. | | |

**Offices held by the Members of the Executive Council, &c.—(*Continued.*)**

| NAMES. | FROM | TO |
|---|---|---|
| VANKOUGHNET, HON. P. M. Member and President of the Executive Council, and Minister of Agriculture.......... | 24th May, 1856, | 29th July, 1858. |
| Member of Executive Council and Commissioner of Crown Lands.................... | 6th August, 1858, | 18th March, 1862. |
| Member of the Legislative Council, for the Rideau Division, elected in 1856. | | |
| VIGER, HON. D. B. Member and president of the Executive Council.......... | 12th December, 1843, | 17th June, 1846. |
| Member of the Legislative Assembly, for Richelieu 1st Parliament, town of Three Rivers 2nd Parliament. | | |
| Member of the Legislative Council............... ...... | 17th February, 1848, | 17th March, 1858. |
| VIGER, HON. L. M. Member of the Executive Council and Receiver General.... | 11th March, 1848, | 26th November, 1849. |
| Member of the Legislative Assembly for Nicolet 1st Parliament, Terrebonne 3rd Parliament, Leinster 4th Parliament. | | |
| WALLBRIDGE, HON. L. Member of the Executive Council and Solicitor General U. C. | 16th May, 1863, | 12th August, 1863. |
| Speaker of the Legislative Assembly.................... | 13th August, 1863, | |
| Member of the Legislative Assembly, for S. R. of Hastings 6th, 7th, and 8th Parliaments. | | |
| WILSON, HON. A. Member of the Executive Council and Solicitor General U. C. | 24th May, 1862, | 10th May, 1863. |
| Member of the Legislative Assembly for N. R. of York 6th and 7th Parliaments. | | |

## Offices held by the Members of the Executive Council, &c.—(Continued.)

| NAMES. | FROM | TO |
|---|---|---|
| YOUNG, HON. J. Member of the Executive Council, Chief Commissioner of Public Works and member of the Board of Railway Commissioners...... Member of the Legislative Assembly for Montreal city, 4th and 5th Parliaments. | 28th October, 1851, | 22nd September, 1852. |

**Alphabetical List of the Members of the Legislative Council appointed by the Crown from 1841 to 1856, when future Members of said Council were made Elective, under Statute 19 & 20 Vict., ch. 140.**

| Names of Members. | L. C. | U. C. | When appointed. | Remarks. |
|---|---|---|---|---|
| Armstrong, D. M. | Hon. | " | | 8th Feby., 1855, | |
| Baldwin, A. | " | " | " | 9th June, 1841, | Resigned on 16th June, 1841. |
| Bolleau, N. F. | " | " | " | 22nd Octr., 1852, | Was Resigned on 31st August, 1850. |
| Berthelot, O. | " | " | " | 9th June, 1841, | Resigned on 28th June, 1851. |
| Boulton, G. S. | " | " | " | 4th June, 1847, | |
| Bourret, Jos. | " | " | " | 21st Novr., 1848, | Died on 5th March, 1859. |
| Bruneau, F. F. | " | " | " | 9th June, 1841, | Died on 4th March, 1851. |
| Caron, R. E. | " | " | " | 9th June, 1841, | He was declared vacated on 16th March, 1857, he having been absent two occasions. Above Resolution not interfered with, 7th May, 1860. |
| Cartier, E. | " | " | " | 8th Feby., 1855, | Died in February, 1858. |
| Crane, S. | " | " | " | 16th Jany., 1849, | His seat declared vacated on 17th March, 1858, for absence. |
| Crookes, Jas. | " | " | " | 9th June, 1841, | Died in 1860. |
| De Beaujeu, G. S. | " | " | " | 21st Novr., 1848, | Died on 29th July, 1865. |
| De Blaquiere, P. B. | " | " | " | 9th June, 1841, | Died in 1860. |
| DeBoucherville, P. B. | " | " | " | 27th Sept., 1843, | Died on 20th November, 1864. |
| Dickson, R. | " | " | " | 19th August, 1842, | Died in 1847. |
| Dickson, W. H. | " | " | " | 8th Feby., 1855, | |
| Dunlop, A. | " | " | " | 19th August, 1842, | Died on 2nd May, 1862. |
| Dumas, Jos. | " | " | " | 19th August, 1842, | Died on 27th December, 1858. |
| Draper, W. H. | " | " | " | 10th April, 1843, | Resigned on 31st January, 1848. |
| Ferguson, A. | " | " | " | 9th June, 1841, | Died in 1862. |
| Ferrie, A. | " | " | " | 9th June, 1841, | Died on 28th December, 1860. |
| Ferrier, Jas. | " | " | " | 27th May, 1847, | |
| Fraser, A. | " | " | " | 9th June, 1841, | Died in 1854. |
| Fraser, J. | " | " | " | 9th June, 1841, | Resigned in 1843. |
| Goodhue, G. J. | " | " | " | 19th August, 1842, | |
| Gosling, J. | " | " | " | 9th Octr., 1845, | Died on 10th April, 1863. |
| Hamilton, Jno. | " | " | " | 9th June, 1841, | |
| Irving, Æ. | " | " | " | 4th Sept., 1843, | Resigned in 1856. |
| Jameson, R. S. | " | " | " | 9th June, 1841, | Resigned on 3rd May, 1850. |
| Joliette, B. | " | " | " | 9th June, 1841, | Died on 21st June, 1850. |
| Jones, R. | " | " | " | 16th Jany., 1849, | Resigned in 1850. |
| Kimber, R. J. | " | " | " | 4th Sept., 1843, | Died shortly after. Never took his seat. |
| Knowlton, P. H. | " | " | " | 9th June, 1841, | Died on 25th August, 1853. |
| Legaré, Jos. | " | " | " | 8th Feby., 1855, | Died on 21st June, 1855. |
| Leslie, Jas. | " | " | " | 23rd May, 1848, | |

## Alphabetical List of the Members of the Legislative Council. &c.—(Con.)

| Names of Members. | | L. C. | U. C. | When appointed. | Remarks. |
|---|---|---|---|---|---|
| Macaulay, J. | Hon. | | " | 9th June, 1841, | Died in 1857. |
| Mason, Lo. | " | ... | " | 4th Sept., 1842, | Resigned in May, 1851. |
| Matheson, R. | " | ... | " | 27th May, 1847, | |
| Maynard, E. | " | ... | " | 9th June, 1841, | Resigned on 22nd June, 1841. |
| McDonald, Jno. | " | ... | " | 9th June, 1841, | His seat vacated, 17th March, 1848. |
| McGill, P. | " | ... | " | 9th June, 1841, | Died in 1860. |
| McKay, T. | " | ... | " | 9th June, 1841, | Died in 1855. |
| Méthot, Le. | " | ... | " | 19th Dec., 1846, | His seat vacated 16th March, 1857. |
| Mills, S. | " | ... | " | 28th Jany., 1849, | |
| Moore, P. H. | " | ... | " | 7th Sept., 1841, | |
| Morris, W. | " | ... | " | 9th June, 1841, | Died on 29th June, 1858. |
| Morris, Jas. | " | ... | " | 27th Novr., 1844, | Died on 29th September, 1865. |
| Neilson, J. | " | ... | " | 25th Novr., 1844, | Died on 1st February, 1848. |
| Panet, Lo. | " | ... | " | 20th Octr., 1852, | |
| Pemberton, G. | " | ... | " | 9th June, 1841, | His seat vacated 29th January, 1849. |
| Perry, E. | " | ... | " | 8th Feby., 1858, | |
| Finlay, H. | " | ... | " | 27th May, 1847, | Died in 1857. |
| Quesnel, J. | " | ... | " | 9th June, 1841, | Died on 29th May, 1842. |
| Quesnel, F. A. | " | ... | " | 8th Sept., 1845, | |
| Ross, Jno. | " | ... | " | 1st Dec., 1848, | |
| Roy, G. | " | ... | " | 14th June, 1841, | Died on 17th December, 1848. |
| Seymour, B. | " | ... | " | 8th Feby., 1858, | |
| Sherwood, L. P. | " | ... | " | 19th August, 1842, | Died on 15th May, 1850. |
| Sullivan, R. B. | " | ... | " | 9th June, 1841, | His seat vacated 30th May, 1851. |
| Taché, J. B. | " | ... | " | 9th June, 1841, | Died on 22nd August, 1849. |
| Taché, E. P. | " | ... | " | 23rd May, 1848, | Died on 30th July, 1865. |
| Turgeon, J. O. | " | ... | " | 28th Dec., 1848, | Died on 9th November, 1856. |
| Viger, D. B. | " | ... | " | 17th Feby., 1848, | His seat vacated 17th March, 1858, died on 13th February, 1861. |
| Walker, W. | " | ... | " | 19th August, 1842, | Died in May, 1862. |
| Washburn, S. | " | ... | " | 19th August, 1842, | Resigned on 8th May, 1844. |
| Widmer, C. | " | ... | " | 15th August, 1842, | Died on 2nd May, 1858. |
| Wilson, C. | " | ... | " | 23rd Octr., 1852, | |
| Wyfie, Jas. | " | ... | " | 29th Jany., 1849, | Died on 6th May, 1854. |

### (*) Alphabetical List of the Members of the Legislative Council of Canada, elected from 1856 to 31st December, 1865.

| Members. | | Electoral Divisions. | U. C. | L. C. | When elected. |
|---|---|---|---|---|---|
| Aikins, J. C. | Hon.... | Home............ | " | | 1862 |
| Alexander, Geo. | " .. | Gore............. | " | | 1858 |
| Allan, G. W. | " .. | York ............ | " | | 1858 |
| Archambault, P. U. | " .. | Repentigny ....... | | " | 1858 |
| Armand, J. F. | " .. | Alma............. | | " | 1858 |
| Baby, F. | " .. | Stadacona........ | | " | 1861 |
| Bennett, T. | " .. | Eastern.......... | " | | 1862 |
| Blair, Fergusson, A. J. | " .. | Brock............ | " | | 1860 |
| Blake, O. | " .. | Thames.......... | " | | 1862 |
| Bossé, J. N. | " .. | De la Durantaye... | | " | 1862 |
| Bull, H. B. | " .. | Burlington ........ | " | | 1864 |
| Bureau, J. O. | " .. | De Lorimier....... | | " | 1862 |
| Burnham, A. A. | " .. | Newcastle........ | " | | 1863 |

(*) See further Contested Elections, &c.

Alphabetical List of the Elected Members of the L. C., &c.—(Con.)

| Members. | | Electoral Divisions. | L. C. | U. C. | When elected. |
|---|---|---|---|---|---|
| Cameron, M. | Hon... | St. Clair............ | | " | 1860 |
| Campbell, A. | " .. | Cataraque.......... | | " | 1858 |
| Chaffers, W. H. | " .. | Rougemont......... | " | | 1864 |
| " " | " .. | " ........ | " | | 1864 |
| Christie, D. | " .. | Erie .............. | | " | 1858 |
| Cormier, C. | " .. | Kennebec ......... | " | | 1862 |
| Crawford, G. | " .. | St. Lawrence...... | | " | 1858 |
| Currie, J. G. | " .. | Niagara........... | | " | 1862 |
| Desaulles, L. A. | " .. | Rougemont........ | " | | 1856 |
| Duchesnay, E. H. J. | " .. | Lauzon .......... | " | | 1856 |
| Duchesnay, E. H. J. | " .. | Lauzon .......... | " | | 1864 |
| Duchesnay, A. J. | " .. | La Salle ......... | " | | 1856 |
| Dumouchel, L. | " .. | Mille Isles........ | " | | 1864 |
| Fergusson Blair, A. J. | " .. | Brock ............ | | " | 1860 |
| Flint, B. | " .. | Trent ............ | | " | 1863 |
| " " | " .. | " ............ | | " | 1864 |
| Foster, A. B. | " .. | Bedford ........... | " | | 1860 |
| Guevremont, J. B. | " .. | Sorel ............ | " | | 1858 |
| Gingras, J. E. | " .. | Stadacona........ | " | | 1864 |
| Hamilton, J. | " .. | Inkerman ........ | " | | 1860 |
| Harwood, R. U. | " .. | Rigaud .......... | " | | 1860 |
| Holton, L. H. | " .. | Victoria.......... | " | | 1862 |
| Huot, P. G. | " .. | Stadacona........ | " | | 1860 |
| Jeffrey, A. | " .. | Newcastle ........ | | " | 1860 |
| Kierskowski, A. E. | " .. | Montarville ....... | " | | 1858 |
| Lacoste, L. | " .. | " ....... | " | | 1861 |
| Lajoie, A. B. | " .. | De Lanaudière..... | " | | 1862 |
| Laterrière, M. P. de Sales | " .. | Laurentides ....... | " | | 1856 |
| Lemieux, F. | " .. | De la Durantaye... | " | | 1862 |
| Leonard, E. | " .. | Malahide ......... | | " | 1862 |
| Letellier de St. Just, L. | " .. | Grandville ........ | " | | 1860 |
| Malhiot, C. | " .. | Shawinegan....... | " | | 1862 |
| Masson, E. | " .. | Mille Isles........ | " | | 1856 |
| Merritt, W. H. | " .. | Niagara........... | | " | 1860 |
| Murney, E. | " .. | Trent............. | | " | 1856 |
| McCrea, W. | " .. | Western .......... | | " | 1862 |
| " " | " .. | " .......... | | " | 1864 |
| McDonald, D. | " .. | Tecumseth......... | | " | 1856 |
| McMaster, W. | " .. | Midland .......... | | " | 1862 |
| McMurrich, J. | " .. | Saugeen .......... | | " | 1862 |
| McNab, Sir A. N. | " .. | Western .......... | | " | 1860 |
| McPherson, D. L. | " .. | Saugeen .......... | | " | 1864 |
| Olivier, L. A. | " .. | De Lanaudière..... | " | | 1863 |
| Patton, J. | " .. | Saugeen .......... | | " | 1856 |
| Price, D. E. | " .. | Laurentides ....... | " | | 1864 |
| Prince, J. | " .. | Western .......... | | " | 1856 |
| Proulx, J. B. | " .. | De la Vallière..... | " | | 1860 |

| Members. | | Electoral Divisions. | L. C. | U. C. | When elected. |
|---|---|---|---|---|---|
| Prudhomme, E. | Hon. ... | Rigaud ............ | " | | 1863 |
| Read, R. | " .. | Quinté............ | | " | 1862 |
| Reesor, D. | " .. | King's............. | | " | 1860 |
| Renaud, Ls. | " .. | De Salaberry...... | " | | 1856 |
| "        " | " .. | "        ....... | | " | 1864 |
| Ryan, Thos. | " .. | Victoria........... | " | | 1863 |
| Sanborn, J. S. | " .. | Wellington........ | " | | " |
| "        " | " .. | "        ......... | | " | 1864 |
| Shaw, Jas. | " .. | Bathurst .......... | | " | 1860 |
| Simpson, J. | " .. | Queen's........... | | " | 1856 |
| Simpson, J. | " .. | "        ......... | | " | 1864 |
| Skead, J. | " .. | Rideau ........... | | " | 1862 |
| "        " | " .. | "        ......... | | " | 1864 |
| Smith, Harmanus | " .. | Burlington ........ | | " | 1856 |
| "    Hollis | " .. | Wellington........ | " | | 1856 |
| "    Sidney | " .. | Trent............. | | " | 1861 |
| Tessier, J. U. | " .. | Gulf............. | " | | 1858 |
| Vankoughnet, P. M. | " .. | Rideau........... | | " | 1856 |
| Vidal, A. | " .. | St. Clair.......... | | " | 1863 |
| Wilson, J. | " .. | "        ......... | | " | " |

# Legislative Council.

*See further Contested Elections, Resignations, &c.*

### 1856 to 1864.

| *Electoral Division.* | *Members Elected.* |
|---|---|
| **L. C.** | **L. C.** |
| De Salaberry.................. | Hon. Ls. Renaud. |
| Laurentides.................... | "  M. P. de S. Laterrière. |
| Lauzon........................ | "  E. H. J. Duchesnay. |
| Mille-Isles.................... | "  E. Masson. |
| Rougemont..................... | "  L. A. Dessaulles. |
| "        .................... | "  W. H. Chaffers. |
| Wellington.................... | "  Hollis Smith. |
| "        .................... | "  J. S. Sanborn. |
| **U. C.** | **U. C.** |
| Burlington.................... | Hon. Harmanus Smith. |
| Queens....................... | "  J. Simpson. |
| Rideau....................... | "  P. M. Vankoughnet. |
| "        .................... | "  J. Skead. |

## Legislative Council—(Continued.)

| Electoral Division. | Members Elected. |
|---|---|
| U. C. | U. C. |
| Saugeen...................... | Hon. J. Patton. |
| " ...................... | " J. McMurrich. |
| Trent...................... | " E. Murney. |
| " ...................... | " Sy. Smith. |
| " ...................... | " B. Flint. |
| Western...................... | " J. Prince. |
| " ...................... | " Sir A. N. MacNab. |
| " ...................... | " W. McCrea. |

### 1858 to 1866.

| L. C. | L. C. |
|---|---|
| Alma...................... | Hon. J. F. Armand. |
| Gulf...................... | " J. U. Tessier. |
| La Salle...................... | " A. J. Duchesnay. |
| Montarville...................... | " A. E. Kierskowski. |
| " ...................... | " L. Lacoste. |
| Repentigny...................... | " P. U. Archambault. |
| Saurel...................... | " J. B. Guevremont. |

| U. C. | U. C. |
|---|---|
| Cataraque...................... | Hon. A. Campbell. |
| Erie...................... | " D. Christie. |
| Gore ...................... | " G. Alexander. |
| St. Lawrence...................... | " G. Crawford. |
| Tecumseth...................... | " D. McDonald. |
| York...................... | " G. W. Allan. |

### 1860 to 1868.

| L. C. | L. C. |
|---|---|
| Bedford...................... | Hon. A. B. Foster. |
| Dela Valière...................... | " J. B. Proulx. |
| Grandville...................... | " L. Letellier de St. Just. |
| Inkerman...................... | " J. Hamilton. |
| Rigaud...................... | " R. U. Harwood. |
| " ...................... | " E. Prudhomme. |
| Stadacona...................... | " P. G. Huot. |
| " ...................... | " F. Baby. |
| " ...................... | " J. E. Gingras. |

| U. C. | U. C. |
|---|---|
| Bathurst...................... | Hon. Jas. Shaw. |
| Brock...................... | " A. J. Ferguson Blair. |
| Kings ...................... | " D. Reesor. |
| Newcastle ...................... | " A. Jeffrey. |
| " ...................... | " A. A. Burnham. |
| Niagara...................... | " W. H. Merritt. |
| " ...................... | " J. G. Currie. |
| St. Clair...................... | " M. Cameron. |
| " ...................... | " J. Wilson. |
| " ...................... | " A. Vidal. |

## Legislative Council,—(*Continued.*)

| *Electoral Division.* | *Members Elected.* |
|---|---|

### 1862 to 1870.

#### L. C.                                         L. C.

| De la Durantaye................ | Hon. F. Lemieux. |
| "        ................ | " J. N. Bossé. |
| De Lanaudiére................ | " A. B. Lajoie. |
| "        ................ | " L. A. Olivier. |
| De Lorimier................ | " J. O. Bureau. |
| Kennebec................ | " C. Cormier. |
| Shawinegan................ | " C. Malhiot. |
| Victoria................ | " L. H. Holton. |
| "        ................ | " Ths. Ryan. |

#### U. C.                                         U. C.

| Eastern................ | Hon. T. Bennett. |
| Home................ | " J. C. Aikins. |
| Malahide................ | " E. Leonard. |
| Midland................ | " W. McMaster. |
| Quinte................ | " R. Read. |
| Thames................ | " O. Blake. |

---

### 1864 to 1872.

#### L. C.                                         L. C.

| De Salaberry................ | Hon. Ls. Renaud. |
| Laurentides................ | " D. E. Price. |
| Lauzon................ | " E. H. Duchesnay. |
| Mille-Isles................ | " L. Dumouchel. |
| Rougemont................ | " W. H. Chaffers. |
| Wellington................ | " J. S. Sanborn. |

#### U. C.                                         U. C.

| Burlington................ | Hon. H. B. Bull. |
| Queens................ | " J. Simpson. |
| Rideau................ | " J. Skead. |
| Saugeen................ | " D. L. McPherson. |
| Trent................ | " B. Flint. |
| Western................ | " W. McCrea. |

---

# LEGISLATIVE COUNCIL.

## Electoral Divisions.

### LOWER CANADA.

Alma.............Part of the County of Hochelaga, part of the Parish of Montreal, the County of Laval, and part of the City of Montreal.

Bedford...........The Counties of Missisquoi, Brome and Shefford.

De la Durantaye..Part of the County of L'Islet, the Counties of Montmagny and Bellechasse and part of the County of Lévi.

De Lanaudière....Part of the County of Maskinongé, and part of the Counties of Berthier and Joliette.

De la Vallière.....The Counties of Nicolet and Yamaska, the Townships of Wendover, Grantham, and that part of Upton which lies in the County of Drummond.

De Lorimier.......The Counties of St. John and Napierville, St. Jean Chrysostôme and Russelltown, in the County of Chateauguay; Hemmingford, in the County of Huntingdon.

De Salaberry.....Part of the County of Chateauguay and of the County of Huntingdon; and the County of Beauharnois.

Grandville ........The Counties of Temiscouata and Kamouraska, and part of the County of L'Islet.

Gulf..............The Counties of Gaspé, Bonaventure and Rimouski.

Inkerman.........The Counties of Argenteuil, Ottawa and Pontiac.

Kennebec.........The Counties of Lotbinière, Megantic and Arthabaska.

La Salle..........Part of the County of Quebec, the County of Portneuf, and part of the Banlieue of Quebec.

Laurentides .......The Counties of Chicoutimi, Charlevoix, Saguenay and Montmorency, and part of the County of Quebec.

Lauzon ...........Part of the County of Lévi, and the Counties of Dorchester and Beauce.

Mille Isles........The Counties of Terrebonne and Two Mountains.

Montarville .......The Counties of Verchères, Chambly and Laprairie.

Repentigny .......Part of the County of Joliette, and the Counties of L'Assomption and Montcalm.

Rigaud ...........Part of the Parish of Montreal, and the Counties of Jacques Cartier, Vaudreuil and Soulanges.

Rougemont .......Part of the County of St. Hyacinthe, and the Counties of Rouville and Iberville.

Saurel............The Counties of Richelieu and Bagot, and part of the County of St. Hyacinthe.

Shawinegan.......The Counties of Champlain and St. Maurice, the Town of Three Rivers, and part of the County of Maskinongé.

Stadacona.........Part of the City and Banlieue of Quebec.

Victoria...........Part of the City of Montreal.

Wellington........Part of the County of Drummond, the County of Richmond, the Town of Sherbrooke, and the Counties of Wolfe Compton and Stanstead.

### UPPER CANADA.

Bathurst ..........The South Riding of Leeds, and the North and South Ridings of Lanark.

Brock ............The North and South Ridings of Wellington, and the North Riding of Waterloo.

## Legislative Council—(*Continued.*)

*Electoral Divisions.*

UPPER CANADA.

Burlington ........The North and South Ridings of Wentworth, and the City of Hamilton.

Cataraque.........The Counties of Addington and Frontenac, and the City of Kingston.

Eastern............The Counties of Stormont, Prescott, Russell, Glengarry, and the Town and Township of Cornwall.

Erie..............The East and West Ridings of Brant, and the County of Haldimand.

Gore .............The South Riding of Waterloo and the North Riding of Oxford.

Home............The Counties of Halton and Peel.

King's............The East and West Ridings of York (except the Township of York) and the South Riding of Ontario.

Malahide..........The East and West Ridings of Elgin, the East Riding of Middlesex, and the City of London.

Midland..........The North Riding of York and the South Riding of Simcoe.

Newcastle........The East Riding of Durham, and the East and West Ridings of Northumberland.

Niagara. ..........The Counties of Lincoln and Welland and the Town of Niagara.

Queen's..........The North Riding of Ontario, the County of Victoria and the West Riding of Durham.

Quinté............The South Riding of Hastings and the County of Prince Edward.

Rideau ...........The Counties of Renfrew and Carleton and the City of Ottawa.

St. Clair..........The County of Lambton and the West Riding of Middlesex.

St. Lawrence......The Town of Brockville and the Township of Elizabethtown, the South Riding of Grenville, the North Riding of Leeds and Grenville and the County of Dundas.

Saugeen ..........The Counties of Bruce and Grey, and the North Riding of Simcoe.

Tecumseth.........The Counties of Huron and Perth.

Thames............The South Riding of Oxford and the County of Norfolk.

Trent..............The County of Peterborough, the N. R. of Hastings and County of Lennox.

Western ..........The Counties of Essex and Kent.

York...............The City of Toronto and the Township of York.

(*) Alphabetical List of the Members of the Legislative Assembly of the
Province of Canada, elected from

1841 to 1865 inclusive.

| Members. | Parlia-ment. | Constituencies. |
|---|---|---|
| Abbott, J. J. C. | 6th | Argenteuil. |
| " | 7 | " |
| " Hon. | 8 | " |
| Aikins, J. C. | 5 | Peel. |
| " | 6 | " |
| Allan, C. | " | Wellington, North Riding. |
| Alleyn, C. | 5 | Quebec, City. |
| " Hon. | 6 | " |
| " " | 7 | " West. |
| " " | 8 | " " |
| Anderson, W. | 7 | Prince Edward. |
| Archambault, A. | 7 | L'Assomption. |
| Archambault, L. | 6 | " |
| " | 8 | " |
| Armstrong, D. M. | 1 | Berthier. |
| " | 2 | " |
| " | 3 | " |
| Ault, S. | 7 | Stormont. |
| " | 8 | " |
| Aylwin, T. C. | 1 | Portneuf. |
| " Hon. | 2 | Quebec, City. |
| " " | 3 | " |
| Baby, M. G. | 5 | Rimouski. |
| " | 6 | " |
| Baby, M. W. | 7 | Temiscouata. |
| Badgley, W. Hon. | 2 | Missisquoi. |
| " | 3 | " |
| " | 4 | Montreal, City. |
| Baldwin, R. Hon. | 1 | Hastings. |
| " | " | York, Fourth Riding. |
| " | " | Rimouski. |
| " | 2 | York, Fourth Riding. |
| " | 3 | " |
| Barthe, J. G. | 1 | Yamaska. |
| Beaubien, J. O. | 6 | Montmagny. |
| " | 7 | " |
| " | 8 | " |
| Beaubien, P. | 1 | Montreal, City. |
| " | 3 | Chambly. |
| Beaudreau, J. | 7 | Richelieu. |
| Bell, R. | 3 | Lanark. |

Alphabetical List of the Members of the Legislative Assembly, &c.—(*Con.*)

| Members. | Parlia-ment. | Constituencies. |
|---|---|---|
| Bell, R.............................. | 5th | Lanark, North Riding. |
| "      .............................. | 6 | "          " |
| "      .............................. | 7 | "          " |
| "      .............................. | 8 | "          " |
| Bell, R.............................. | 7 | Russell. |
| "      .............................. | 8 | " |
| Bellerose, J. H...................... | 8 | Laval. |
| Bellingham, S....................... | 5 | Argenteuil. |
| "      .............................. | 6 | " |
| Benjamin, Geo....................... | 5 | N. R. of Hastings. |
| "      .............................. | 6 | " |
| "      .............................. | 7 | " |
| Benoit, P........................... | 7 | Napierville. |
| Berthelot, A........................ | 1 | Kamouraska. |
| "      .............................. | 2 | " |
| Bertrand, Ls........................ | " | Rimouski. |
| Biggar, H........................... | 5 | Brant, West Riding. |
| "      .............................. | 6 | " |
| Biggar, J. L........................ | 7 | Northumberland, E. R. |
| "      .............................. | 8 | " |
| Black, H............................ | 1 | Quebec, City. |
| Blair, (*see* Fergusson)............. |   | |
| Blake, W. H......................... | 3 | York, East Riding. |
| Blanchet, J......................... | 5 | Quebec, City. |
| Blanchet, **J. G**................... | 7 | **Levis.** |
| "      .............................. | 8 | " |
| Borne, **M**......................... | 1 | Rimouski. |
| Boswell, **G. M**.................... | 1 | Northumberland, South Riding. |
| Boucher de Boucherville, C.......... | 7 | Chambly. |
| "      .............................. | 8 | " |
| Boucher de Niverville............... | " | Three Rivers, City. |
| Boulton, H. J....................... | 1 | Niagara, Town. |
| "      .............................. | 3 | Norfolk. |
| Boulton, W. H....................... | 2 | Toronto, City. |
| "      .............................. | 3 | " |
| "      .............................. | 4 | " |
| Bourassa, F......................... | 5 | St. Johns, Town. |
| Bourassa, F., Jr.................... | 6 | " |
| "      .............................. | 7 | " |
| "      .............................. | 8 | " |
| **Bouthillier**, T.................. | 1 | St. Hyacinthe. |
| "      .............................. | 2 | " |
| "      .............................. | 3 | " |
| Bowes, J. G......................... | 5 | Toronto, City. |
| Bowman, J. E........................ | 8 | Waterloo, North Riding. |
| Bown, J. Y.......................... | 7 | E. R., Brant. |
| "      .............................. | 8 | " |

Alphabetical List of the Members of the Legislative Assembly, &c.—(Con.)

| Members. | Parliament. | Constituencies. |
|---|---|---|
| Brodeur, T......................... | 5th | Bagot. |
| Brooks, S.......................... | 2 | Sherbrooke, County. |
|     "     ...................... | 3 | " |
| Brousseau, J. D................... | 7 | Portneuf. |
|     "     .................. | 8 | " |
| Brown, G.......................... | 4 | Kent. |
|     "     ...................... | 5 | Lambton. |
|     "     ...................... | 6 | Oxford, North Riding. |
|     "     ...................... | " | Toronto, City. |
|     "   Hon............... | 7 | Oxford, South Riding. |
|     "    "  ............... | 8 | " |
| Buchanan, Isaac................... | 1 | City of Toronto. |
|     "     ............... | 6 | City of Hamilton. |
|     "     ............... | 7 | " |
|     "     ............... | 8 | " |
| Bureau, J. O...................... | 5 | Napierville. |
|     "     ............... | 6 | " |
|     "     ............... | 7 | " |
| Burnet, D ........................ | 1 | Quebec, City. |
| Burnham, A. A.................... | 4 | Northumberland. |
| Burritt R.......................... | 3 | Grenville. |
| Burton, F. H...................... | 5 | Durham, East Riding. |
|     "     ............... | 6 | " |
| Burwell, L........................ | 6 | E. R., Elgin. |
|     "     ............... | 7 | " |
|     "     ............... | 8 | " |
| Cameron, J........................ | 6 | Victoria. |
| Cameron, J. H.................... | 2 | Cornwall, Town. |
|     "     ............... | 3 | " |
|     "     ............... | 5 | Toronto, City. |
|     "   Hon............... | 7 | Peel. |
|     "    "  ............... | 8 | " |
| Cameron, Malcolm................ | 1 | Lanark. |
|     "     ............... | 2 | " |
|     "     ............... | 3 | Kent. |
|     "   Hon............... | 4 | Huron. |
|     "    "  ............... | 6 | Lambton. |
| Cameron, M. C.................... | 7 | Ontario, North Riding. |
|     "     ............... | 8 | " |
| Campbell, E. C.................... | 1 | Niagara, Town. |
| Campbell, T. E.................... | 6 | Rouville. |
| Carling, J......................... | " | London, City. |
|     "     ............... | 7 | " |
|     "   **Hon** ............... | 8 | " |
| Caron, G.......................... | 6 | Maskinongé. |
|     "     ............... | 7 | " |

## Alphabetical List of the Members of the Legislative Assembly, &c.—(Con.)

| Members. | Parlia-ment. | Constituencies. |
|---|---|---|
| Caron, L. B. | 6th | L'Islet. |
| " | S | " |
| Carroll, P. | 3 | Oxford. |
| Cartier, G. E. | " | Verchères. |
| " | 4 | " |
| " | 5 | " |
| " Hon | 6 | " |
| " " | 7 | Montreal, City, East. |
| " " | 8 | " |
| Cartwright, J S. | 1 | Lennox and Addington. |
| Cartwright, R. J. | 8 | " |
| Casault, N | 5 | Montmagny. |
| Cauchon, J. | 2 | Montmorenci. |
| " | 3 | " |
| " | 4 | " |
| " | 5 | " |
| " Hon | 6 | " |
| " " | 7 | " |
| " " | 8 | " |
| Cayley, W., Hon | 2 | Huron. |
| " | 3 | " |
| " | 5 | Huron and Bruce. |
| " | 6 | Renfrew. |
| Chabot, J. | 1 | Quebec, City. |
| " | 2 | " |
| " | 3 | " |
| " Hon | 4 | Bellechasse. |
| " " | 5 | " |
| " " | 5 | Quebec, City. |
| Chaffers, W. H. | 5 | Rouville. |
| Chalmers, G. | 2 | Halton, East Riding. |
| Chambers, F. W. | 8 | Town of Brockville. |
| Chapais, J. C. | 4 | Kamouraska. |
| " | 5 | " |
| " | 6 | " |
| " | 7 | " |
| " Hon | 8 | " |
| Chauveau, P. J O. | 2 | Quebec, County. |
| " | 3 | " |
| " | 4 | " |
| " | 5 | " |
| Chesley, S. Y. | 1 | Cornwall, Town. |
| Childs, M. | 1 | Stanstead. |
| Chisholm, J. K. | 5 | Halton. |
| Christie, D. | 4 | Wentworth. |
| " | 5 | Brant, East Riding. |
| " | 6 | " |

| Members. | Parlia-ment. | Constituencies. |
|---|---|---|
| Christie, R........................ | 1st | Gaspé. |
| " | 2 | " |
| " | 3 | " |
| " | 4 | " |
| Church, B. R.................... | 5 | Leeds & Grenville, North Riding. |
| " | 6 | " |
| Cimon, C......................... | " | Charlevoix. |
| Clapham, J. G................... | 4 | Megantic. |
| Clarke, J. R..................... | 6 | Northumberland, East Riding. |
| Clarke, W....................... | 5 | Wellington, North Riding. |
| " | 7 | " |
| Cockburn, Jas.................... | 7 | Northumberland, W. R. |
| " Hon............ | 8 | " |
| Colville, E....................... | 2 | Beauharnois. |
| Conger, R. B..................... | " | Prince Edward. |
| Conger, W. S..................... | 5 | Peterborough. |
| " | 8 | " |
| Connor, S........................ | 6 | Oxford, South Riding. |
| " | 7 | " |
| Cook, E.......................... | 5 | Oxford, South Riding. |
| Cook, J.......................... | 1 | Dundas. |
| Cook, J. W....................... | 6 | " |
| Cooke, A......................... | 5 | Ottawa, County. |
| Corneillier dit Grandchamp, H....... | 8 | Joliette. |
| Coupal dit Lareine, S.............. | 8 | Napierville. |
| Coutlée, D. A.................... | 6 | Soulanges. |
| Cowan, J......................... | 7 | Waterloo, South Riding. |
| " | 8 | " |
| Craik, R......................... | 6 | Middlesex, E. R. |
| Crane, S......................... | 1 | Grenville. |
| Crawford, G...................... | 4 | Brockville, Town. |
| " | 5 | " |
| Crawford, J...................... | 7 | Toronto City, (East.) |
| Crysler, J. P.................... | 3 | Dundas. |
| " | 5 | " |
| Cummings, Jas.................... | 2 | Lincoln, South Riding. |
| Currier, J. M.................... | 8 | Ottawa, City. |
| Cuthbert, W...................... | 3 | Bonaventure. |
| Cuvillier, A..................... | 1 | Huntingdon. |
| Daly, D., Hon.................... | 1 | Megantic. |
| " | 2 | " |
| " | 3 | " |
| Daly, T. M....................... | 5 | Perth. |
| " | 6 | " |
| " | 7 | " |
| Daoust, C........................ | 5 | Beauharnois. |

5*

Alphabetical List of the Members of the Legislative Assembly, &c.—(*Con.*)

| Members. | Parliament. | Constituencies. |
|---|---|---|
| Daoust, **J. B**. | 5th | Two Mountains. |
| " | 6 | " |
| " | 7 | " |
| " | 8 | " |
| Darche, N. | 5 | Chambly. |
| Davignon, P. | 3 | Rouville. |
| Dawson, W. M. | 6 | Three Rivers, City. |
| " | 7 | Ottawa, County. |
| Day, C. D. | 1 | " |
| De Bleury, C. C. S. | 2 | Montreal, City. |
| De Cazes, Chs. | 7 | Richmond and Wolfe. |
| Delisle, A. M. | 1 | Montreal, County. |
| Delong, J. | 4 | Leeds. |
| " | 5 | Leeds, South Riding. |
| **Denis**, P. | 7 | Beauharnois. |
| " | 8 | " |
| De Niverville, (*see* Boucher) | | |
| Derbishire, S. | 1 | Bytown. |
| De Salaberry, M. A. | " | Rouville. |
| Desaulniers, F. | 2 | St. Maurice. |
| Desaulniers, L. L. L. | 5 | " |
| " | 6 | " |
| " | 7 | " |
| Desrivières, **H**. | 1 | Verchères. |
| De Witt, J. | " | Leinster. |
| " | 2 | " |
| " | 3 | Beauharnois. |
| " | 5 | Chateauguay. |
| Dickson, J. | 7 | Huron and Bruce. |
| " | 8 | " |
| Dickson, **W**. H. | 2 | Niagara Town. |
| " | 3 | " |
| Dixon, T. C. | 4 | London, Town. |
| Dionne, **B** | 5 | Témiscouata. |
| " | 6 | " |
| Dorion, A. A. | 5 | Montreal, City. |
| " | 6 | " |
| " Hon. | 7 | Hochelaga. |
| " " | 8 | " |
| Dorion, J. B. E. | 5 | Drummond and Arthabaska. |
| " | 7 | " |
| " | 8 | " |
| Dorland, W. C. | 6 | Prince Edward. |
| Dostaler, P. E. | 5 | Berthier. |
| Draper, W. H. | 1 | Russell. |
| " Hon. | 2 | London, Town. |
| Drummond, L. T. | " | Portneuf. |

## Alphabetical List of the Members of the Legislative Assembly, &c.—(Con.)

| Members. | Parliament. | Constituencies. |
|---|---|---|
| Drummond, L .T........................ | 3rd | Shefford. |
| " ........................ | 4 | " |
| " Hon................ | 5 | " |
| " ........................ | 6 | " |
| " ........................ | " | Lothinière. |
| " ........................ | 7 | Rouville. |
| Dubord, H.......................... | 4 | Quebec, City. |
| " .......................... | 6 | " |
| Duchesnay, A. J.................... | 3 | Portneuf. |
| Duckett, W........................ | 8 | Soulanges. |
| Dufresne, A....................... | 7 | Iberville. |
| " ....................... | 8 | " |
| Dufresne, J....................... | 5 | Montcalm. |
| " ....................... | 6 | " |
| " ....................... | 7 | " |
| " ....................... | 8 | " |
| Duggan, G. Jr..................... | 1 | York, Second Riding. |
| " ..................... | 2 | " |
| Dumas, N......................... | 3 | Leinster. |
| Dumoulin, P. B.................... | 4 | Yamaska. |
| Dunkin, C........................ | 6 | Drummond and Arthabaska. |
| " ........................ | 7 | Brome. |
| " ........................ | 8 | " |
| Dunlop, Wm....................... | 1 | Huron. |
| " ....................... | 2 | " |
| Dunn, Hon. J. H.................. | 1 | Toronto, City. |
| Dunscomb, J. W.................. | 1 | Beauharnois. |
| Dunsford, J. W.................. | 7 | Victoria. |
| " .................. | 8 | " |
| Durand, Jas...................... | 1 | Halton, West Riding. |
| Egan, J.......................... | 3 | Ottawa, County. |
| " .......................... | 4 | " |
| " .......................... | 5 | Pontiac. |
| Ermatinger, E.................... | 2 | Middlesex. |
| Evanturel, F..................... | 5 | Quebec, County. |
| " ..................... | 7 | " |
| " Hon.................. | 8 | " |
| Falkner, J. P.................... | 7 | Hochelaga. |
| Fellowes, G. B. L. (See Lyon)..... | 6 | Russell. |
| Felton, W. L..................... | 5 | Sherbrooke and Wolfe. |
| Fergusson, A. J.................. | 3 | Waterloo. |
| " .................. | 4 | " |
| " .................. | 5 | Wellington, South Riding. |
| Ferguson, T. R.................. | 6 | Simcoe, South Riding. |
| " .................. | 7 | " |
| " .................. | 8 | " |

| Members. | Parlia-ment. | Constituencies. |
|---|---|---|
| Ferguson, **W**. | 8th | Frontenac. |
| Ferres, J. **M**. | 5 | Missisquoi, East Riding. |
| " | 6 | Brome. |
| Ferrie, **R**. | 5 | Waterloo, South Riding. |
| Finlayson, **H**. | 6 | Brant, East Riding. |
| Flint, B. | 3 | Hastings. |
| " | 5 | "    South Riding. |
| Foley, M. H. | " | Waterloo, North Riding. |
| " | 6 | " |
| " Hon. | 7 | Perth. |
| "    " | " | Waterloo, North Riding. |
| "    " | 8 | " |
| Forbes, C. J. | 1 | Two Mountains. |
| Fortier, M. | 7 | Yamaska, |
| " | 8 | " |
| **Fortier, O. C**. | 5 | Bellechasse. |
| " | 6 | " |
| Fortier, T. | 3 | Nicolet. |
| " | 4 | " |
| " | 5 | " |
| Foster, A. B. | 6 | Shefford. |
| Foster, S. S. | 1 | " |
| " | 2 | " |
| **Fournier, C. F**. | " | L'Islet. |
| " | 3 | " |
| " | 4 | " |
| " | 5 | " |
| " | 6 | " |
| " | 7 | " |
| Franchère, T. | 1 | Rouville. |
| " | 2 | " |
| Frazer, J. | 5 | Welland. |
| Freeman, S. B. | " | Wentworth, South Riding. |
| Gagnon, A. | 7 | Charlevoix. |
| " | 8 | " |
| Galt, A. T. | 3 | Sherbrooke, County. |
| " | 4 | "    Town. |
| " | 5 | "    " |
| " Hon. | 6 | "    " |
| "    " | 7 | "    " |
| "    " | 8 | "    " |
| Gamble, J. W. | 4 | York, South Riding. |
| "    " | 5 | "  West Riding. |
| Gaucher, G. G. | 8 | Jacques Cartier, |
| Gaudet, J. | 6 | Nicolet. |
| "    " | 7 | " |
| "    " | 8 | " |

## Alphabetical List of the Members of the Legislative Assembly, &c.—(Con.)

| Members. | Parliament. | Constituencies. |
|---|---|---|
| Gauvreau, L. H.............. | 6th | Maskinongé, |
| Geoffrion, F. ................ | 8 | Verchères. |
| Gibbs, T. N. ................ | 8 | Ontario, South Riding. |
| Gilchrist, J. ................ | 1 | Northumberland, North Riding. |
| Gill, J. ................ | 5 | Yamaska. |
| "  " ................ | 6 | |
| Gouin, A. N. ................ | 4 | Richelieu. |
| Gould, J. ................ | 5 | Ontario, North Riding. |
| "  " ................ | 6 | " |
| Gowan, O. R. ................ | 2 | Leeds. |
| "  " ................ | 6 | Leeds & Grenville, North Riding. |
| Grieve, E. ................ | 2 | Three Rivers, Town. |
| Guevremont, J. B. ................ | 5 | Richelieu. |
| Gugy, B. C. A. ................ | 3 | Sherbrooke, Town. |
| Guillet, L. ................ | 2 | Champlain. |
| "  " ................ | 3 | " |
| | | |
| Hale, E. ................ | 1 | Sherbrooke, Town. |
| "  " ................ | 2 | " |
| Hall, G. B. ................ | " | Northumberland, South Riding. |
| "  J. ................ | 3 | Peterborough. |
| Hamilton, J. R. ................ | 6 | Bonaventure. |
| Harcourt, M. ................ | 6 | Haldimand. |
| "  " ................ | 7 | " |
| Harrison, S. B. Hon. ................ | 1 | Kingston, City. |
| "  "  " ................ | 2 | Kent. |
| Hartman, J. ................ | 4 | York, North Riding. |
| "  " ................ | 5 | " |
| " ................ | 6 | " |
| Harwood, R. U., Hon. ................ | 6 | Vaudreuil. |
| Harwood, A. C. D. ................ | 8 | Vaudreuil. |
| Haultain, F. W. ................ | 7 | Peterborough. |
| "  " ................ | 8 | " |
| Heath, E. ................ | 6 | Pontiac. |
| Hebert, N. ................ | " | Megantic. |
| "  " ................ | 7 | " |
| Higginson, T. ................ | 8 | Prescott. |
| Hincks, F. ................ | 1 | Oxford. |
| "  "  Hon. ................ | 3 | " |
| "  "  " ................ | 4 | Niagara, Town. |
| "  "  " ................ | " | Oxford. |
| "  "  " ................ | 5 | " South Riding. |
| "  "  " ................ | 5 | Renfrew. |
| Hogan, J. S. ................ | 6 | Grey. |
| Holmes, B. ................ | 1 | Montreal, City. |
| "  " ................ | 3 | " |
| "  J. ................ | 6 | Huron & Bruce. |
| Holton, L. H. ................ | 5 | Montreal City. |

## Alphabetical List of the Members of the Legislative Assembly, &c.—(Con.)

| Members. | Parliament. | Constituencies. |
|---|---|---|
| Holton, L. H. Hon................... | 8th | Chateaugay. |
| Hooper, A. F....................... | 7 | Lennox & Addington. |
| Hopkins, C........................ | 1 | Halton, East Riding. |
| "        "........................ | 3 | Halton. |
| Houde, M.......................... | 8 | Maskinongé. |
| Howland, W. P..................... | 6 | York, West Riding. |
| "        " Hon................. | 7 | " |
| "        "   "................. | 8 | " |
| Huntington, L. S. ................ | 7 | Shefford. |
| "        "   Hon.............. | 8 | " |
| Huot, P. G........................ | 5 | Saguenay. |
| "        "........................ | 6 | Quebec City, East. |
| "        "........................ | 7 | " |
| "        "........................ | 8 | " |
| **Irvine, G.**....................... | **8** | Megantic. |
| Jackson, Geo...................... | 5 | Grey. |
| "        "...................... | 7 | " |
| "        "...................... | 8 | " |
| **Jessup, H. D.**..................... | 2 | Grenville. |
| **Jobin, A.**....................... | 1 | Montreal, County. |
| "        "...................... | 2 | " |
| "        "...................... | 3 | " |
| Jobin, J. H....................... | 4 | Berthier. |
| "        "...................... | 5 | Joliette. |
| "        "...................... | 6 | " |
| "        "...................... | 7 | " |
| Johnson, T. H..................... | 3 | Prescott. |
| "        "..................... | 4 | " |
| Johnston, J....................... | 1 | Carleton. |
| "        "....................... | 2 | " |
| Joly, H. G........................ | 7 | Lotbinière. |
| "        "........................ | 8 | " |
| Jones, D. F....................... | 8 | Leeds, South Riding. |
| Jones, F.......................... | 7 | Leeds & Grenville, North Riding. |
| "        "......................... | 8 | " |
| **Jones, R.**....................... | 1 | Missisquoi. |
| **Judah, H.**....................... | " | Champlain. |
| Kierskowski, **A. E.**................. | 7 | Verchères. |
| Killaly, H. H..................... | 1 | London, Town. |
| Kimber, R. J...................... | " | Champlain. |
| Knight, A......................... | 7 | Stanstead. |
| "        ....................... | 8 | " |

Alphabetical List of the Members of the Legislative Assembly, &c.—(Con.)

| Members. | Parliament. | Constituencies. |
|---|---|---|
| Labelle, P. | 5th | Laval. |
| " | 6 | " |
| " | 7 | " |
| Laberge, C. J. | 5 | Iberville. |
| " | 6 | " |
| Labrèche-Viger L. | 7 | Terrebonne. |
| " | 8 | " |
| Lacoste, L. | 1 | Chambly. |
| " | 2 | " |
| " | 3 | " |
| " | 4 | " |
| " | 6 | " |
| Lafontaine, L. H. | 1 | York, Fourth Riding. |
| " Hon | 2 | Terrebonne. |
| " " | 3 | Terrebonne. |
| " " | 3 | Montreal, City. |
| Laframboise, M. | 6 | Bagot. |
| " | 7 | " |
| " | 8 | " |
| Lajoie, C. | 8 | St. Maurice. |
| Langevin, H. L. | 6 | Dorchester. |
| " | 7 | " |
| " | 8 | " |
| Langton, J. | 4 | Peterborough. |
| " | 5 | " |
| Lantier, J. P. | 2 | Vaudreuil. |
| Laporte, J. | 5 | Montreal, Hochelaga Riding. |
| do | 6 | Hochelaga, County. |
| Larwill, E. | 5 | Kent. |
| LaTerrière, M. P. D. | 2 | Saguenay. |
| " | 3 | " |
| " | 4 | " |
| Lawrason, L. | 2 | London, Town. |
| Laurin, J. | 2 | Lotbinière. |
| " | 3 | " |
| " | 4 | " |
| LeBlanc, O. | 4 | Beauharnois. |
| LeBoutillier, D. | 4 | Bonaventure. |
| LeBoutillier, J. | 2 | |
| " | 5 | Gaspé. |
| " | 6 | " |
| " | 7 | " |
| " | 8 | " |
| Lemieux, F. | 2 | Dorchester. |
| " | 3 | " |
| " | 4 | " |
| " | 5 | Levis. |
| " Hon. | 6 | " |

## Alphabetical List of the Members of the Legislative Assembly, &c.—(*Con.*)

| Members. | Parlia-ment. | Constituencies. |
|---|---|---|
| Lemoine, **B. H.** | 2nd | Huntingdon. |
| Leslie, J. | 1 | Verchères. |
| " | 2 | " |
| " | 3 | " |
| Letellier, L. | 3 | Kamouraska. |
| Leveillé, M. F. | 3 | Yamaska. |
| Loranger, T. J. J. | 5 | Laprairie. |
| " | 6 | " |
| " Hon | 7 | " |
| Loux, J. W. | 6 | Russell. |
| Lumsden, J. M. | 5 | Ontario, South Riding. |
| Lyon, G. | 2 | Carleton. |
| Lyon, G. B. | 3 | Russell. |
| " | 4 | " |
| " (see Fellowes) | 5 | " |
| | | |
| Magill, Charles | 8 | Hamilton, City. |
| Malloch, E. | 3 | Carleton. |
| " | 4 | " |
| Manahan, A. | 1 | Kingston. |
| Marchildon, T. | 4 | Champlain. |
| " | 5 | " |
| Marquis, P. C. | 3 | Kamouraska. |
| Martin, J. L. | 7 | Montcalm. |
| Masson, L. H. | 5 | Soulanges. |
| Matheson, D. | 5 | Oxford, North Riding. |
| Mattice, W. | 4 | Stormont. |
| " | 5 | " |
| Mattice, **W. D.** | 6 | " |
| Meagher, **J.** | 5 | Bonaventure. |
| " | 6 | " |
| Merritt, W. H. | 1 | Lincoln, North Riding. |
| " | 2 | " " |
| " | 3 | Lincoln. |
| " Hon | 4 | " |
| " | 5 | " |
| " | 6 | " |
| Méthot, A. P. | 2 | Nicolet. |
| Méthot, F. X. | 3 | Quebec City. |
| Meyers, A. H. | 2 | Northumberland, North Riding. |
| " | 3 | Northumberland. |
| Moffatt, **G.** Hon. | 1 | Montreal, City. |
| " | 2 | " " |
| Mongenais, **J.** B. | 3 | Vaudreuil. |
| " | 4 | " |
| " | 5 | " |
| " | 6 | " |
| " | 7 | " |

## Alphabetical List of the Members of the Legislative Assembly, &c.—(Con.)

| Members. | Parliament. | Constituencies. |
|---|---|---|
| Mouro, G. | 2nd | York, Third Riding. |
| Moore, J. | 1 | Sherbrooke, County. |
| Morin, A. N. | 1 | Nicolet. |
| " | 1 | Saguenay. |
| " Hon. | 2 | Bellechasse. |
| " | " | Saguenay. |
| " | 3 | Bellechasse. |
| " | 4 | Terrebonne. |
| " | 5 | Chicoutimi and Tadoussac. |
| Morin, L. S. | * | Terrebonne. |
| " | 6 | " |
| " Hon. | 7 | Laval. |
| Morris, A. | 7 | Lanark, South Riding. |
| " | 8 | " |
| Morris, J. | 1 | Leeds. |
| Morrison, A. | 5 | Simcoe, North Riding. |
| " | 6 | " |
| " | 7 | |
| " | 8 | Niagara, Town. |
| Morrison, J. C. | 3 | York, West Riding. |
| " | 4 | Niagara, Town. |
| " | 5 | " |
| Morton, J. | 7 | Frontenac. |
| Mowat, O. | 6 | Ontario, South Riding. |
| " Hon. | 7 | " |
| " " | 8 | " |
| Munro, H. | 5 | Durham, West Riding. |
| " | 6 | " |
| " | 7 | " |
| " | 8 | " |
| Murney, E. | 1 | Hastings. |
| " | 2 | " |
| " | 4 | " |
| " | 5 | Hastings, North Riding. |
| Macbeth, G. | 5 | Elgin, West Riding. |
| " | 6 | " |
| " | 7 | " |
| McCann, H. W. | 5 | Prescott. |
| " | 6 | " |
| " | 7 | " |
| McConkey, T. D. | 8 | Simcoe, North Riding. |
| McConnell, J. | 2 | Stanstead. |
| " | 3 | " |
| McCulloch, M. | 1 | Terrebonne. |
| Macdonald, A. P. | 6 | Maskinongé, West Riding. |
| Macdonald, D. | 1 | Prescott. |
| Macdonald, D. A. | 6 | Glengarry. |
| " | 7 | " |
| " | 8 | " |

| Members. | Parliament. | Constituencies. |
|---|---|---|
| McDonell, D. E. | 2nd | Stormont. |
| McDonell, G. | " | Dundas. |
| Macdonald, J. | 8 | Toronto City, (West.) |
| Macdonald, J. A. | 2 | Kingston, City |
| "           Hon. | 3 | " |
| "      " | 4 | " |
| "      " | 5 | " |
| "      " | 6 | " |
| "      " | 7 | " |
| "      " | 8 | " |
| Macdonald, J. S. | 1 | Glengarry. |
| " | 2 | " |
| " | 3 | " |
| " | 4 | " |
| "      Hon. | 5 | " |
| "      " | 6 | Cornwall, Town. |
| "      " | 7 | " |
| "      " | 8 | " |
| Macdonald, R. | 2 | Cornwall. |
| " | 4 | Cornwall Town. |
| " | 5 | " |
| McDougald, J. L. | 6 | Renfrew. |
| McDougall, J. | 4 | Drummond. |
| McDougall, W. | 6 | Oxford, North Riding. |
| "      Hon. | 7 | " |
| " | 8 | Ontario, North Riding. |
| " | " | Lanark, North Riding. |
| McFarland, D. | 3 | Welland. |
| Macfarlane, R. | 8 | Perth. |
| McGee, T. D. | 6 | Montreal, City. |
| " | 7 | "      West |
| "      Hon. | 8 | "      " |
| McGiverin, W. | 8 | Lincoln. |
| McIntyre, R. | " | Renfrew. |
| McKellar, A. | 6 | Kent. |
| " | 7 | " |
| " | 8 | " |
| Mackenzie, A. | 7 | Lambton. |
| " | 8 | " |
| Mackenzie, H. F. | 6 | " |
| " | 8 | Oxford, North Riding. |
| Mackenzie, W. L. | 3 | Haldimand. |
| " | 4 | " |
| " | 5 | " |
| " | 6 | " |
| McKerlie, D. | 5 | Brant, East Riding. |
| McLachlin, D. | 4 | Bytown. |
| " | 7 | Renfrew. |

## Alphabetical List of the Members of the Legislative Assembly, &c.—(Con.)

| Members. | Parliament. | Constituencies. |
|---|---|---|
| McLean, A. | 1st | Stormont. |
| " | 8 | " |
| McLeod, J. | 6 | Essex. |
| McMicken, G. | " | Welland. |
| McMonies, J. | 8 | Wentworth, North Riding. |
| McNab, A. N. | 1 | Hamilton, City. |
| " Sir | 2 | Hamilton. |
| " " | 3 | " |
| " " | 4 | " |
| " " | 5 | " |
| | | |
| Neilson, J. | 1 | Quebec, County. |
| Nelson, W. | 2 | Richelieu. |
| " | 3 | " |
| Niles, Wm. | 5 | Middlesex, East Riding. |
| Niverville, (see Boucher) | | |
| Noel, J. B. J. | 1 | Lotbinière. |
| Notman, Wm. | 3 | Middlesex. |
| " | 6 | Wentworth, North Riding |
| " | 7 | " |
| " | 8 | " |
| | | |
| O'Connor, J. | 7 | Essex. |
| O'Farrell, J. | 5 | Lotbinière. |
| " | 6 | " |
| Ogden, C. R. | 1 | Three Rivers, Town. |
| O'Halloran, Jas. | 7 | Missisquoi. |
| " | 8 | " |
| Ouimet, G. | 6 | Beauharnois. |
| | | |
| Paige, S. | 4 | Missisquoi. |
| Painchand, C. F. | 7 | Verchères. |
| Panet, Chs. | 6 | Quebec, County. |
| Papin, J. | 5 | L'Assomption. |
| Papineau, D. B. | 1 | Ottawa, County. |
| " Hon. | 2 | " |
| Papineau, D. E. | 6 | " |
| Papineau, L. J. | 3 | St. Maurice. |
| " Hon. | 4 | Two Mountains. |
| Paquet, A. H. | 8 | Berthier. |
| Parent, E. | 1 | Saguenay. |
| Parke, T. | " | Middlesex. |
| Parker, T. S. | 8 | Wellington, North Riding. |
| Patrick, W. | 4 | Grenville. |
| " | 5 | Grenville, South Riding. |
| " | 6 | " |
| " | 7 | " |

## Alphabetical List of the Members of the Legislative Assembly, &c.—(Con.)

| Members. | Parliament. | Constituencies. |
|---|---|---|
| Perreault, J. F.. | 8th | Richelieu. |
| Perry, P. | 3 | York, East Riding. |
| Petrie, A. | 2 | Russell. |
| Piché, E. U. | 6 | Berthier. |
| Pinsonneault, A. | 7 | Laprairie. |
| " | 8 | " |
| **Playfair, A. W.** | 6 | Lanark, South Riding. |
| **Polette, A.** | 3 | Three Rivers, Town. |
| " | 4 | " |
| " | 5 | " |
| Pope, J. H. | 6 | Compton. |
| " | 7 | " |
| " | 8 | " |
| Portman, M. P., Hon. | 7 | Middlesex, East Riding. |
| Poulin, J. N. | 4 | Rouville. |
| " | 5 | " |
| " | 8 | " |
| Pouliot, B. | 5 | Dorchester. |
| Pouliot, J. B. | 8 | Temiscouata. |
| Poupore, J. | 7 | Pontiac. |
| " | 8 | " |
| Powell, J. W. | 1 | Norfolk. |
| " | 2 | " |
| Powell, Wm. | 6 | " |
| Powell, W. F. | 5 | Carleton. |
| " | 6 | " |
| " | 7 | " |
| " | 8 | " |
| Prevost, G. M. | 5 | Terrebonne. |
| Prevost, J. B. J. | 7 | Soulanges. |
| Price, D. E. | 5 | Chicoutimi and Tadoussac. |
| " | 6 | Chicoutimi and Saguenay. |
| " | 7 | " |
| " | 8 | " |
| Price, J. H. | 1 | York, First Riding. |
| " | 2 | " |
| " | 3 | York, South Riding. |
| Prince, J. | 1 | Essex. |
| " | 2 | " |
| " | 3 | " |
| " | 4 | " |
| **Purdy, J. T.** | 6 | Grey. |
| **Queshel, F. A.** | 1 | Montmorenci. |
| Rankin, A. | 5 | Essex. |
| " | 7 | " |
| " | 8 | " |

| Members. | Parliament | Constituencies. |
|---|---|---|
| Raymond, J. M. | 1st | Leinster. |
| Raymond, R. | 8 | St. Hyacinthe. |
| Remillard, E. | 7 | Bellechasse. |
| " | 8 | " |
| Rhodes, Wm. | 5 | Megantic. |
| Richards, A. N. | 8 | Leeds, South Riding. |
| Richards, W. B. | 3 | Leeds. |
| " Hon. | 4 | " |
| Riddell, R. | 2 | Oxford. |
| Ridout, G. P. | 4 | Toronto, City. |
| Robertson, C. | 1 | Two Mountains. |
| Robinson, J. B., Jr. | 6 | Toronto, City. |
| " Hon. | 7 | " (West.) |
| Robinson, W. B. | 2 | Simcoe. |
| " | 3 | " |
| " | 4 | " |
| " | 5 | " South Riding. |
| Robitaille, T. | 7 | Bonaventure. |
| " | 8 | " |
| Roblin, D. | 5 | Lennox & Addington. |
| " | 6 | " |
| Roblin, J. P. | 1 | Prince Edward. |
| " | 2 | " |
| Rolph, J. Hon. | 4 | Norfolk. |
| " " | 5 | " |
| Rose, J. | 6 | Montreal, City. |
| " Hon. | 7 | " Centre. |
| " " | 8 | " " |
| Rose, J. W. | 4 | Dundas. |
| Ross, D. | 3 | Megantic. |
| " | 5 | Beauce. |
| " | 6 | " |
| Ross, Jas. | 5 | Northumberland, East Riding. |
| " | 6 | Wellington, North Riding. |
| Ross, J. J. | 7 | Champlain. |
| " | 8 | " |
| Ross, J. S. | 7 | Dundas. |
| " | 8 | " |
| Ross, W. | " | Prince Edward. |
| Rousseau, L. | 2 | Yamaska. |
| Ruel, A. G. | 1 | Bellechasse. |
| Ryerson, W. | 7 | Brant, West Riding. |
| Rykert, J. C. | 6 | Lincoln. |
| " | 7 | " |
| Rymal, J. | 6 | Wentworth, South Riding. |
| " | 7 | " |
| " | 8 | " |

## Alphabetical List of the Members of the Legislative Assembly, &c.—(Con.)

| Members. | Parlia-ment. | Constituencies. |
|---|---|---|
| Sanborn, **J. S** | 3rd | Sherbrooke, County. |
| " | 4 | " |
| " | 5 | Compton. |
| Sauvageau, **T** | 3 | Huntingdon. |
| Scatcherd, J | 5 | Middlesex, West Riding. |
| " | 6 | " |
| " | 7 | " |
| " | 8 | " |
| Scoble, **J** | 7 | Elgin, West Riding. |
| " | 8 | " |
| Scott, J | 3 | Bytown. |
| Scott, R. W | 6 | Ottawa, City. |
| " | 7 | " |
| Scott, W | 6 | Waterloo, South Riding. |
| Scott, W. F | 2 | Two Mountains. |
| " | 3 | " |
| " | 4 | " |
| Seymour, B | 2 | Lennox & Addington. |
| " | 3 | " |
| " | 4 | " |
| Shanly, W | 8 | Grenville, South Riding. |
| Shaw, Jas | 4 | Lanark. |
| " | 5 | Lanark, South Riding. |
| Sherwood, G | 1 | Brockville, Town. |
| " | 2 | " |
| " | 3 | " |
| " | 6 | " |
| " Hon | 7 | " |
| Sherwood, H. " | 1 | Toronto, City. |
| " " | 2 | " |
| " " | 3 | " |
| " " | 4 | " |
| Short, E | " | Sherbrooke, Town. |
| Short, T | 6 | Peterborough. |
| Sicotte, L. V | 4 | St. Hyacinthe. |
| " | 5 | " |
| " | 6 | " |
| " Hon | 7 | " |
| " " | 8 | " |
| Simard, **G. H** | 5 | Quebec, City. |
| " | 6 | " |
| " | 7 | " Centre. |
| Simpson, **J** | 1 | Vaudreuil. |
| " | 6 | Niagara, Town. |
| " | 7 | " |
| " **Hon** | 8 | " |
| Sincennes, **J. F** | 6 | Richelieu. |

## Alphabetical List of the Members of the Legislative Assembly, &c.—(Con.)

| Members. | Parliament. | Constituencies. |
|---|---|---|
| Small, J. E................................ | 1st | York, Third Riding. |
| " Hon........................ | 2 | " |
| Smith, A. M............................. | 8 | Toronto, City, (East.) |
| Smith, Har............................. | 1 | Wentworth. |
| " ................................ | 2 | " |
| " ................................ | 3 | " |
| Smith, Henry........................... | 1 | Frontenac. |
| " ................................ | 2 | " |
| " ................................ | 3 | " |
| " ................................ | 4 | " |
| " ................................ | 5 | " |
| " ................................ | 6 | " |
| Smith, Jas. Hon..................... | 2 | Missisquoi. |
| " ................................ | 3 | Durham. |
| " ................................ | 4 | " |
| " ................................ | 5 | Victoria. |
| Smith, J. S............................. | 7 | Durham, East Riding. |
| " ................................ | 8 | " |
| Smith, Sidney......................... | 5 | Northumberland, West Riding. |
| " ................................ | 6 | " |
| Somerville, R. B..................... | 5 | Huntingdon. |
| " ................................ | 6 | " |
| " ................................ | 7 | " |
| " ................................ | 8 | " |
| Southwick, G.......................... | 5 | Elgin, East Riding. |
| Spence, R............................... | 4 | Wentworth, North Riding. |
| Starnes, H............................. | 6 | Chateaugai. |
| " ................................ | 7 | " |
| Steele, E................................ | 1 | Simcoe. |
| Stevenson, D. B...................... | 3 | Prince Edward. |
| " ................................ | 4 | " |
| " ................................ | 5 | " |
| Stewart, N............................. | 2 | Prescott. |
| Stewart, Wm.......................... | 4 | Bytown. |
| Stuart, G. O........................... | 4 | Quebec, City. |
| " ................................ | 5 | " |
| Stuart, Wm............................ | 1 | Russell. |
| Stirton, D.............................. | 6 | Wellington, South Riding. |
| " ................................ | 7 | " |
| " ................................ | 8 | " |
| Strachan, J. M........................ | 1 | York, Third Riding. |
| Street, T. C............................ | 4 | Welland. |
| " ................................ | 7 | " |
| " ................................ | 8 | " |
| Supple, J................................ | 5 | Renfrew. |
| Sweet, M................................ | 7 | Brome. |
| Sylvain, Geo........................... | 7 | Rimouski. |
| " ................................ | 8 | " |

6

| Members. | Parliament. | Constituencies. |
| --- | --- | --- |
| Taché, E. P. | 1st | L'Islet. |
| " | 2 | " |
| Taché, J. C. | 3 | Rimouski. |
| " | 4 | " |
| " | 5 | " |
| Talbot, M. | 6 | Middlesex, East Riding. |
| Taschereau, A. C. | 1 | Dorchester. |
| Taschereau, H. E. | 7 | Beauce. |
| " | 8 | " |
| Taschereau, J. A. | 2 | Dorchester. |
| Taschereau, P. E. | " | " |
| Tassé, F. Z. | 6 | Jacques Cartier. |
| " | 7 | " |
| " | 8 | " |
| Terrill, H. B. | 4 | Stanstead. |
| Terrill, T. L. | " | " |
| " | 5 | " |
| " Hon. | 6 | " |
| Tessier, U. J. | 4 | Portneuf. |
| Tett, B. | 6 | Leeds, South Riding. |
| " | 7 | " |
| Thibaudeau, J. E. | 5 | Portneuf. |
| " | 6 | " |
| Thibaudeau, Isid. Hon. | 8 | Quebec City, Centre. |
| Thompson, D. | 1 | Haldimand. |
| " | 2 | " |
| " | 3 | " |
| " | 8 | " |
| Thorburn, D. | 1 | Lincoln, South Riding. |
| Tremblay, P. A. | 8 | Chicoutimi and Saguenay. |
| Turcotte, J. E. | 1 | St. Maurice. |
| " | 4 | " |
| " | 5 | Maskinongé. |
| " | 6 | Champlain. |
| " | 7 | Three Rivers, City. |
| " Hon. | 8 | " |
| Turgeon, A. | 1 | Bellechasse. |
| Valois, M. F. | 4 | Montreal, County. |
| " | 5 | Montreal, Jacques Cartier Riding. |
| Varin, J. B. | 4 | Huntingdon. |
| Viger, D. B. | 1 | Richelieu. |
| " Hon. | 2 | Three Rivers, Town. |
| Viger, L. M. | 1 | Nicolet. |
| " | 3 | Terrebonne. |
| " | 4 | Leinster. |

## Alphabetical List of the Members of the Legislative Assembly, &c.—(Con.)

| Members. | Parlia-ment. | Constituencies. |
|---|---|---|
| Wakefield, E. G. | 1st | Beauharnois. |
| Walker, Wm. | " | Rouville. |
| Wallbridge, L. | 6 | Hastings, South Riding. |
| " | 7 | " |
| " Hon. | 8 | " |
| Wallbridge, T. C. | 8 | Hastings, North Riding. |
| Walsh, A. | 7 | Norfolk. |
| " | 8 | " |
| Watts, R. N. | 1 | Drummond. |
| " | 2 | " |
| " | 3 | " |
| Webb, W. H. | 6 | Richmond & Wolfe. |
| " | 8 | " |
| Webster, Jas. | 2 | Halton, West Riding. |
| " | 3 | Waterloo. |
| Wells, J. P. | 8 | York, North Riding. |
| Wetenhall, J. | 3 | Halton. |
| White, J. | 4 | " |
| " | 6 | " |
| " | 7 | " |
| " | 8 | |
| Whitney, H. H | 5 | Missisquoi, West Riding. |
| " | 6 | " |
| Wilson, A. Hon. | 6 | York, North Riding. |
| " | 7 | " |
| Willson, C. | 4 | Middlesex. |
| " | 8 | Middlesex, East Riding. |
| Wilson, J. | 2 | London, Town. |
| " | 3 | " |
| " | 5 | " |
| Williams, J. T. | 1 | Durham. |
| " | 2 | " |
| Wood, E. B. | 8 | Brant, West Riding. |
| Woods, J. | 1 | Kent. |
| " | 2 | |
| Wright, Alonzo. | 8 | Ottawa, County. |
| Wright, Amos. | 4 | York, East Riding. |
| " | 5 | " |
| " | 6 | " |
| " | 7 | " |
| " | 8 | " |
| Wright, G. | 4 | York, West Riding. |
| Yielding, A. | 5 | Bytown. |
| Young, J. Hon. | 4 | Montreal, City. |
| " | 5 | " |
| Yule, J. Jr. | 1 | Chambly. |

# (1) LEGISLATIVE ASSEMBLY.

## FIRST PARLIAMENT.

*8th April, 1841, to 23rd September, 1844.*

**84 Members—42 for each section of the Province.**

| Constituencies. | L. C. | U. C. | Members. |
|---|---|---|---|
| Beauharnois.................... | " |  | J. W. Dunscomb. |
| " .................... | " |  | E. G. Wakefield. |
| Bellechasse................... | " |  | A. G. Ruel. |
| " .................... | " |  | A. Turgeon. |
| Berthier...................... | " |  | D. M. Armstrong. |
| Bonaventure................... | " |  | J. R. Hamilton. |
| Brockville.................... |  | " | G. Sherwood. |
| Bytown....................... |  | " | S. Derbishire. |
| Carleton..................... |  | " | Jas. Johnston. |
| Chambly...................... | " |  | J. Yule, Jr. |
| " .................... | " |  | L. Lacoste. |
| Champlain.................... | " |  | R. J. Kimber. |
| " .................... | " |  | H. Judah. |
| Cornwall..................... |  | " | S. Y. Chesley. |
| Dorchester................... | " |  | A. C. Taschereau. |
| Drummond.................... | " |  | R. N. Watts. |
| Dundas ...................... |  | " | J. Cook. |
| Durham...................... |  | " | J. T. Williams. |
| Essex........................ |  | " | J. Prince. |
| Frontenac.................... |  | " | H. Smith, Jr. |
| Gaspé........................ | " |  | R. Christie. |
| Glengarry.................... |  | " | J. S. Macdonald. |
| Grenville.................... |  | " | S. Crane. |
| Haldimand................... |  | " | D. Thompson. |
| Halton, E. R................. |  | " | C. Hopkins. |
| Halton, W. R................. |  | " | J. Durand. |
| Hamilton, City............... |  | " | A. N. MacNab. |
| Hastings .................... |  | " | Hon. R. Baldwin. |
| " .................... |  | " | E. Murney. |
| Huntingdon .................. | " |  | A. Cuvillier. |
| Huron....................... |  | " | J. M. Strachan. |
| " .................... |  | " | W. Dunlop. |
| Kamouraska.................. | " |  | A. Berthelot. |
| Kent........................ |  | " | J. Woods. |
| Kingston, City............... |  | " | A. Manahan. |
| " .................... |  | " | Hon. S. B. Harrison. |
| Lanark...................... |  | " | M. Cameron. |
| Leeds....................... |  | " | Jas. Morris. |

(1) See further Contested Elections, Special Elections, &c.

## Legislative Assembly—(Continued.)

| Constituencies. | L. C. | U. C. | Members. |
|---|---|---|---|
| Leinster | " | | J. M. Raymond. |
| " | " | | J. De Witt. |
| Lennox and Addington | | " | J. S. Cartwright. |
| Lincoln, N. R. | | " | W. H. Merritt. |
| Lincoln, S. R. | | " | D. Thorburn. |
| L'Islet | " | | E. P. Taché. |
| London, Town | | " | H. H. Killaly. |
| Lotbinière | " | | J. B. J. Noël. |
| Megantic | " | | Hon. D. Daly. |
| Middlesex | | " | T. Parke. |
| Missisquoi | " | | R. Jones. |
| Montmorenci | " | | F. A. Quesnel. |
| Montreal, City | " | | Hon. G. Moffatt. |
| " | " | | B. Holmes. &. |
| " | " | | P. Beaubien. |
| Montreal, County | " | | A. M. Delisle. |
| " | " | | A. Jobin. |
| Niagara, Town | | " | E. C. Campbell. |
| " | | " | H. J. Boulton. |
| Nicolet | " | | A. N. Morin. |
| " | " | | L. M. Viger. |
| Norfork | | " | J. W. Powell. |
| Northumberland, S. R. | | " | G. M. Boswell. |
| Northumberland, N. R. | | " | J. Gilchrist. |
| Ottawa, County | " | | C. D. Day. |
| " | " | | D. B. Papineau. |
| Oxford | | " | F. Hincks. |
| Portneuf | " | | T. C. Aylwin. |
| Prescott | | " | D. Macdonald. |
| Prince Edward | | " | J. P. Roblin. |
| Quebec, City | " | | D. Burnet. |
| " | " | | H. Black. |
| " | " | | J. Chabot. |
| Quebec, County | " | | J. Neilson. |
| Richelieu | " | | D. B. Viger. |
| Rimouski | " | | M. Borne. |
| " | " | | Hon. R. Baldwin. |
| Rouville | " | | M. A. DeSalaberry. |
| " | " | | Wm. Walker. |
| " | " | | T. Franchère. |
| Russell | | " | W. H. Draper. |
| " | | " | W. Stuart. |
| Saguenay | " | | E. Parent. |
| " | " | | Hon. A. N. Morin. |
| Shefford | * | | S. S. Foster. |
| Sherbrooke, Town | " | | E. Hale. |
| " County | " | | J. Moore. |

| Constituencies. | L. C. | U. C. | Members. |
|---|---|---|---|
| Simcoe | | " | E. Steele. |
| Stanstead | " | | M. Child. |
| Stormont | | " | A. McLean. |
| St. Hyacinthe | " | | T. Boutillier. |
| St. Maurice | " | | J. E. Turcotte. |
| Terrebonne | " | | M. McCulloch. |
| Three Rivers, Town | " | | C. R. Ogden. |
| Toronto, City | | " | Hon. J. H. Dunn. |
| " | | " | J. Buchanan. |
| " | | " | Hon. H. Sherwood. |
| Two Mountains | " | | C. Robertson. |
| " | " | | C. J. Forbes. |
| Vaudreuil | " | | J. Simpson. |
| Verchères | " | | H. Desrivières. |
| " | " | | J. Leslie. |
| Wentworth | | " | Harm. Smith. |
| Yamaska | " | | J. G. Barthe. |
| York, First Riding | | " | J. H. Price. |
| York, Second Riding | | " | G. Duggan, Jr. |
| York, Third Riding | | " | J. E. Small. |
| York, Fourth Riding | | " | R. Baldwin. |
| " | | " | L. H. LaFontaine. |

# SECOND PARLIAMENT.

12th *November*, 1844, *to* 6th *December*, 1847.

**84 Members—42 for each section of the Province.**

| Constituencies. | L. C. | U. C. | Members. |
|---|---|---|---|
| Beauharnois | " | | E. Colville. |
| Bellechasse | " | | Hon. A. N. Morin. |
| Berthier | " | | D. M. Armstrong. |
| Bonaventure | " | | J. LeBoutillier. |
| Brockville | | " | G. Sherwood. |
| Bytown | | " | W. Stewart. |
| Carleton | | " | J. Johnston. |
| " | | " | G. Lyon. |
| Chambly | " | | L. Lacoste. |
| Champlain | " | | L. Guillet. |

## Legislative Assembly—(Continued.)

| Constituencies. | L. C. | U. C. | Members. |
|---|---|---|---|
| Cornwall | | " | R. Macdonald. |
| " | | " | J. H. Cameron. |
| Dorchester | " | | F. E. Taschereau. |
| " | " | | J. A. Taschereau. |
| " | " | | P. Lemieux. |
| Drummond | " | | R. N. Watts. |
| Dundas | | " | G. Macdonell. |
| Durham | | " | J. T. Williams. |
| Essex | | " | J. Prince. |
| Frontenac | | " | Henry Smith. |
| Gaspé | " | | R. Christie. |
| Glengarry | | " | J. S. Macdonald. |
| Grenville | | " | H. D. Jessup. |
| Haldimand | | " | D. Thompson. |
| Halton, E. R. | | " | G. Chalmers. |
| Halton, W. R. | | " | J. Webster. |
| Hamilton, City | | " | Sir A. N. MacNab. |
| Hastings | | " | E. Murney. |
| Huntingdon | " | | B. H. LeMoine. |
| Huron | | " | W. Dunlop. |
| " | | " | Hon. W. Cayley. |
| Kamouraska | " | | A. Berthelot. |
| Kent | | " | Hon. S. B. Harrison. |
| " | | " | J. Woods. |
| Kingston, City | | " | J. A. Macdonald. |
| Lanark | | " | M. Cameron. |
| Leeds | | " | O. R. Gowan. |
| Leinster | " | | J. DeWitt. |
| Lennox and Addington | | " | B. Seymour. |
| Lincoln, N. R. | | " | W. H. Merritt. |
| Lincoln, S. R. | | " | J. Cummings. |
| L'Islet | " | | E. P. Taché. |
| " | " | | C. F. Fournier. |
| London, Town | | " | L. Lawrason. |
| " | | " | Hon. W. H. Draper. |
| " | | " | J. Wilson. |
| Lotbinière | " | | J. Laurie. |
| Megantic | " | | Hon. D. Daly. |
| Middlesex | | " | E. Ermatinger. |
| Missisquoi | " | | Hon. Jas. Smith. |
| " | " | | Hon. W. Badgley. |
| Montmorenci | " | | J. Cauchon. |
| Montreal, City | * | | Hon. G. Moffatt. |
| " | * | | C. C. S. DeBleury. |
| Montreal, County | * | | A. Jobin. |
| Niagara, Town | | * | W. H. Dickson. |
| Nicolet | * | | A. P. Methot. |

## Legislative Assembly—(*Continued.*)

| Constituencies. | L. C. | U. C. | Members. |
|---|---|---|---|
| Norfolk | | " | J. W. Powell. |
| Northumberland, S. R. | | " | G. B. Hall. |
| Northumberland, N. R. | | " | A. H. Meyers. |
| Ottawa, County | " | | Hon. D. B. Papineau. |
| Oxford | | " | R. Riddell. |
| Portneuf | " | | L. T. Drummond. |
| Prescott | | " | N. Stewart. |
| Prince Edward | | " | J. P. Roblin. |
| " | | " | R. B. Conger. |
| Quebec, City | " | | Hon. T. C. Aylwin. |
| " | " | | J. Chabot. |
| Quebec, County | " | | P. J. O. Chauveau. |
| Richelieu | " | | W. Nelson. |
| Rimouski | " | | L. Bertrand. |
| Rouville | " | | T. Franchère. |
| Russell | | " | A. Petrie. |
| Saguenay | " | | Hon. A. N. Morin. |
| " | " | | M. P. D. Laterrière. |
| Shefford | " | | S. S. Foster. |
| Sherbrooke, Town | " | | Edw. Hale. |
| " County | " | | S. Brooks. |
| Simcoe | | " | W. B. Robinson. |
| Stanstead | " | | J. McConnell. |
| Stormont | | " | D. Æ. Macdonell. |
| St. Hyacinthe | " | | T. Boutillier. |
| St. Maurice | " | | F. Desaulniers. |
| Terrebonne | " | | Hon. L. H. LaFontaine. |
| Three Rivers, Town | " | | Edw. Grieve. |
| " | " | | Hon. D. B. Viger. |
| Toronto, City | | " | Hon. H. Sherwood. |
| " | | " | W. H. Boulton. |
| Two Mountains | " | | W. H. Scott. |
| Vaudreuil | " | | J. P. Lantier. |
| Verchères | " | | J. Leslie. |
| Wentworth | | " | Har. Smith. |
| Yamaska | " | | L. Rousseau. |
| York, First Riding | | " | J. H. Price. |
| " Second " | | " | G. Duggan. |
| " Third " | | " | Hon. J. E. Small. |
| " " | | " | G. Monro. |
| " Fourth | | " | Hon. R. Baldwin. |

# THIRD PARLIAMENT.

24th January, 1848, to 6th November, 1851.

## 84 Members—42 for each section of the Province.

| Constituencies. | L. C. | U. C. | Members. |
|---|---|---|---|
| Beauharnois.................... | " | | J. DeWitt. |
| Bellechasse.................... | " | | Hon. A. N. Morin. |
| Berthier...................... | " | | D. M. Armstrong. |
| Bonaventure ................. | " | | W. Cuthbert. |
| Brockville.................... | | " | G. Sherwood. |
| Bytown....................... | | " | J. Scott. |
| Carleton..................... | | " | E. Malloch. |
| Chambly..................... | " | | P. Beaubien. |
| " ...................... | " | | L. Lacoste. |
| Champlain ................... | " | | L. Guillet. |
| Cornwall, Town.............. | | " | Hon. J. H. Cameron. |
| Dorchester.................. | " | | F. Lemieux. |
| Drummond................... | " | | R. N. Watts. |
| Dundas ..................... | | " | J. P. Chrysler. |
| Durham...................... | | " | Jas. Smith. |
| Essex ...................... | | " | J. Prince. |
| Frontenac................... | | " | H. Smith. |
| Gaspé ...................... | " | | E. Christie. |
| Glengarry................... | | " | J. S. Macdonald. |
| Grenville ................... | | " | R. Burritt. |
| Haldimand .................. | | " | D. Thompson. |
| " .................. | | " | W. L. Mackenzie. |
| Halton...................... | | " | J. Wetenhall. |
| " ...................... | | " | C. Hopkins. |
| Hamilton City............... | | " | Sir A. N. MacNab. |
| Hastings .................... | | " | B. Flint. |
| Huntingdon ................. | " | | T. Sauvageau. |
| Huron ...................... | | " | Hon. W. Cayley. |
| Kamouraska.................. | " | | P. C. Marquis. |
| " .................. | " | | L. Letellier. |
| Kent ....................... | | " | M. Cameron. |
| Kingston, City............... | | " | Hon. J. A. Macdonald. |
| Lanark ..................... | | " | R. Bell. |
| Leeds ...................... | | " | W. B. Richards. |
| Leinster .................... | " | | N. Dumas. |
| Lennox & Addington.......... | | " | B. Seymour. |
| Lincoln ..................... | | " | W. H. Merritt. |
| L'Islet ..................... | " | | C. F. Fournier. |
| London, Town............... | | " | J. Wilson. |
| Lotbinière.................. | " | | J. Laurin. |

## Legislative Assembly—(*Continued*.)

| Constituencies. | L. C. | U. C. | Members. |
|---|---|---|---|
| Megantic | " | | Hon. D. Daly. |
| " | " | | D. Ross. |
| Middlesex | | " | W. Notman. |
| Missisquoi | " | | Hon. W. Badgley. |
| Montmorenci | " | | J. Cauchon. |
| Montreal, City | " | | Hon. L. H. LaFontaine. |
| " " | " | | B. Holmes. |
| " County | " | | A. Jobin. |
| Niagara, Town | | " | W. H. Dickson. |
| Nicolet | " | | T. Fortier. |
| Norfolk | | " | Hon. H. J. Boulton. |
| Northumberland | | " | A. H. Meyers. |
| Ottawa, County | | " | J. Egan. |
| Oxford | | " | P. Carroll. |
| " | | " | Hon. F. Hincks. |
| Peterborough | | " | Jas. Hall. |
| Portneuf | " | | A. J. Duchesnay. |
| Prescott | | " | T. H. Johnson. |
| Prince Edward | | " | D. B. Stevenson. |
| Quebec, City | " | | Hon. T. C. Aylwin, |
| " | " | | J. Chabot. |
| " | " | | F. X. Méthot. |
| " County | " | | P. J. O. Chauveau. |
| Richelieu | " | | W. Nelson. |
| Rimouski | " | | J. C. Taché. |
| Rouville | " | | P. Davignon. |
| Russell | | " | G. B. Lyon. |
| Saguenay | " | | Hon. M. P. D. Laterrière. |
| Shefford | " | | L. T. Drummond. |
| Sherbrooke, Town | " | | B. C. A. Gugy. |
| " County | " | | S. Brooks. |
| " " | " | | A. T. Galt. |
| " " | " | | J. S. Sanborn. |
| Simcoe | | " | W. B. Robinson. |
| Stanstead | " | | J. McConnell. |
| Stormont | | " | A. McLean. |
| St. Hyacinthe | " | | T. Boutillier. |
| St. Maurice | " | | L. J. Papineau. |
| Terrebonne | " | | Hon. L. H. Lafontaine. |
| " | " | | Hon. L. M. Viger. |
| Toronto, City | | " | Hon. H. Sherwood. |
| " " | | " | W. H. Boulton. |
| Three Rivers, Town | " | | A. Polette. |
| Two Mountains | " | | W. H. Scott. |
| Vaudreuil | " | | J. B. Mongenais. |
| Verchères | " | | Jas. Leslie. |
| " | " | | G. E. Cartier. |

## Legislative Assembly—(Continued.)

| Constituencies. | L. C. | U. C. | Members. |
|---|---|---|---|
| Wentworth...................... | | " | Har. Smith. |
| Waterloo ...................... | | " | J. Webster. |
| " ...................... | | " | A. J. Ferguson. |
| Welland ...................... | | " | D. McFarland. |
| Yamaska...................... | " | | M. F. Leveillé. |
| York, N. R....................... | | " | Hon. R. Baldwin. |
| " E. R....................... | | " | W. H. Blake. |
| " E. R....................... | | " | F. Perry. |
| " S. R....................... | | " | J. H. Price. |
| " W. R....................... | | " | J. C. Morrison. |

## FOURTH PARLIAMENT.

*24th December*, 1851, *to 23rd June*, 1854.

**84 Members—42 for each section of the Province.**

| Constituencies. | L. C. | U. C. | Members. |
|---|---|---|---|
| Beauharnois ...................... | " | | O. Leblanc. |
| Bellechasse...................... | " | | Hon. J. Chabot. |
| Berthier ...................... | " | | J. H. Jobin. |
| Bonaventure ...................... | " | | D. LeBoutillier. |
| Brockville, Town...................... | | " | G. Crawford. |
| Bytown " ...................... | | " | D. McLachlin. |
| Carleton ...................... | | " | E. Malloch. |
| Chambly...................... | " | | L. Lacoste. |
| Champlain ...................... | " | | T. Marchildon. |
| Cornwall, Town...................... | | " | R. Macdonald. |
| Dorchester ...................... | " | | F. Lemieux. |
| Drummond...................... | " | | J. McDougall. |
| Dundas ...................... | | " | J. W. Rose. |
| Durham ...................... | | " | J. Smith. |
| Essex...................... | | " | J. Prince. |
| Frontenac...................... | | " | H. Smith. |
| Gaspé ...................... | " | | R. Christie. |
| Glengarry...................... | | " | J. S. Macdonald. |
| Grenville...................... | | " | W. Patrick. |
| Haldimand...................... | | " | W. L. Mackenzie. |
| Halton...................... | | " | J. White. |
| Hamilton, City...................... | | | Sir A. N. MacNab. |
| Hastings...................... | | | E. Murney. |

## Legislative Assembly—(Continued.)

| Constituencies. | L. C. | U. C. | Members. |
|---|---|---|---|
| Huntingdon | " | | J. B. Varin. |
| Huron | | " | Hon. M. Cameron. |
| Kamouraska | " | | J. C. Chapais. |
| Kent | | " | Geo. Brown. |
| Kingston, City | | " | Hon. J. A. Macdonald. |
| Lanark | | " | Jas. Shaw. |
| Leeds | | " | Hon. W. B. Richards. |
| " | | " | J. Delong. |
| Leinster | " | | Hon. L. M. Viger. |
| Lennox and Addington | | " | B. Seymour. |
| Lincoln | | " | Hon. W. H. Merritt. |
| L'Islet | " | | C. F. Fournier. |
| London Town | | " | T. C. Dixon. |
| Lotbinière | " | | J. Laurin. |
| Megantic | " | | J. G. Clapham. |
| Middlesex | | " | C. Willson. |
| Missisquoi | " | | S. Paige. |
| Montmorenci | " | | J. Cauchon. |
| Montreal, City | " | | Hon. J. Young. |
| " " | " | | Hon. W. Badgley. |
| " County | " | | M. F. Valois. |
| Niagara, Town | | " | Hon. F. Hincks. |
| " | | " | J. C. Morrison. |
| Nicolet | " | | T. Fortier. |
| Norfolk | | " | Hon. J. Rolph. |
| Northumberland | | " | A. A. Burnham. |
| Ottawa, County | " | | J. Egan. |
| Oxford | | " | Hon. F. Hincks. |
| Peterborough | | " | J. Langton. |
| Portneuf | " | | U. J. Tessier. |
| Prescott | | " | T. H. Johnson. |
| Prince Edward | | " | D. B. Stevenson. |
| Quebec, City | " | | G. O. Stuart. |
| " " | " | | H. Dubord. |
| " County | " | | P. J. O. Chauveau. |
| Richelieu | " | | A. N. Gouin. |
| Rimouski | " | | J. C. Taché. |
| Rouville | " | | J. N. Poulin. |
| Russell | | " | G. B. Lyon. |
| Saguenay | " | " | Hon. M. P. D. Laterrière. |
| Shefford | " | | Hon. L. T. Drummond. |
| Sherbrooke, Town | " | | Edw. Short. |
| " " | " | | A. T. Galt. |
| " County | " | | J. S. Sanborn. |
| Simcoe | | " | W. B. Robinson. |
| Stanstead | " | | H. B. Terrill. |
| " | " | | T. L. Terrill. |

## Legislative Assembly—(*Continued.*)

| Constituencies. | L. C. | U. C. | Members. |
|---|---|---|---|
| Stormont | | " | W. Mattice. |
| St. Hyacinthe | " | | L. V. Sicotte. |
| St. Maurice | " | | J. E. Turcotte. |
| Terrebonne | " | | Hon. A. N. Morin. |
| Three Rivers, Town | " | | A. Polette. |
| Toronto City | | " | G. P. Ridout. |
| " | | " | W. H. Boulton. |
| " | | " | Hon. H. Sherwood. |
| Two Mountains | " | | W. H. Scott. |
| " | " | | Hon. L. J. Papineau. |
| Vaudreuil | " | | J. B. Mongenais. |
| Vercheres | " | | G. E. Cartier. |
| Waterloo | | " | A. J. Fergusson. |
| Welland | | " | T. C. Street. |
| Wentworth | | " | D. Christie. |
| Yamaska | " | | P. B. Dumoulin. |
| York, N. R. | | " | J. Hartman. |
| " S. R. | | " | J. W. Gamble. |
| " E. R. | | " | Amos Wright. |
| " W. R. | | " | G. Wright. |

## FIFTH PARLIAMENT.

*10th August, 1854, to 28th November, 1857.*

**130 Members—65 for each section of the Province.**

| Constituencies. | L. C. | U. C. | Members. |
|---|---|---|---|
| Argenteuil | * | | S. Bellingham. |
| Bagot | * | | T. Brodeur. |
| Beauce | * | | D. Ross. |
| Beauharnois | " | | Chs. Daoust. |
| Bellechasse | " | | Hon. J. Chabot. |
| " | " | | O. C. Fortier. |
| Berthier | " | | P. E. Dostaler. |
| Bonaventure | " | | J. Meagher. |
| Brant, E. R. | | " | D. McKerlie. |
| " " | | " | D. Christie. |
| " W. R. | | " | H. Biggar. |
| Brockville, Town | | " | G. Crawford. |
| Bytown, Town | | * | A. Yielding. |
| Carleton | | * | W. F. Powell. |

## Legislative Assembly—(Continued.)

| Constituencies. | L. C. | U. C. | Members. |
|---|---|---|---|
| Chambly | " | | N. Darche. |
| Champlain | " | | T. Marchildon. |
| Chateaugai | " | | J. DeWitt. |
| Chicoutimi and Tadoussac | " | | Hon. A. N. Morin. |
| " | " | | D. E. Price. |
| Compton | " | | J. S. Sanborn. |
| Cornwall, Town | | " | R. Macdonald. |
| Dorchester | " | | B. Pouliot. |
| Drummond and Arthabaska | " | | J. B. E. Dorion. |
| Dundas | | " | J. P. Crysler. |
| Durham, E. R. | | " | F. H. Burton. |
| " W. R. | | " | H. Munro. |
| Elgin, E. R. | | " | G. Southwick. |
| " W. R. | | " | G. Macbeth. |
| Essex | | " | A. Rankin. |
| Frontenac | | " | H. Smith. |
| Gaspé | " | | J. LeBoutillier. |
| Glengarry | | " | Hon. J. S. Macdonald. |
| Grenville, S. R. | | " | W. Patrick. |
| Grey | | " | G. Jackson. |
| Haldimand | | " | W. L. Mackenzie. |
| Halton | | " | G. K. Chisholm. |
| Hamilton, City | | " | Sir A. N. MacNab, Kt. |
| Hastings, N. R. | | " | E. Murney. |
| " N. R. | | " | G. Benjamin. |
| " S. R. | | " | B. Flint. |
| Huntingdon | " | | R. B. Somerville. |
| Huron and Bruce | | " | Hon. W. Cayley. |
| Iberville | " | | C. J. Laberge. |
| Joliette | " | | J. H. Jobin. |
| Kamouraska | " | | J. C. Chapais. |
| Kent | | " | E. Larwill. |
| Kingston, City | | " | Hon. J. A. Macdonald. |
| Lambton | | " | Geo. Brown. |
| Lanark, N. R. | | " | R. Bell. |
| " S. R. | | " | Jas. Shaw. |
| Laprairie | " | | T. J. J. Loranger. |
| L'Assomption | " | | J. Papin. |
| Laval | " | | P. Labelle. |
| Leeds and Grenville, N. R. | | " | B. R. Church. |
| Leeds, S. R. | | " | J. Delong. |
| Lennox and Addington | | " | D. Roblin. |
| Levis | " | | F. Lemieux. |
| Lincoln | | " | Hon. W. H. Merritt. |
| L'Islet | " | | C. F. Fournier. |
| London, Town | | " | J. Wilson. |
| Lotbinière | " | | J. O'Farrell. |

## Legislative Assembly—(Continued.)

| Constituencies. | L. C. | U. C. | Members. |
|---|---|---|---|
| Maskinongé | " | | J. E. Turcotte. |
| Megantic | " | | W. Rhodes. |
| Middlesex E. R. | | " | Wm. Niles. |
| " W. R. | | " | J. Scatcherd. |
| Missisquoi, E. R. | " | | J. M. Ferres. |
| " W. R. | " | | H. H. Whitney. |
| Montcalm | " | | J. Dufresne. |
| Montmagny | " | | N. Casault. |
| Montmorenci | " | | J. Casshon. |
| Montreal, City | " | | A. A. Dorion. |
| " " | " | | L. H. Holton. |
| " " | " | | Hon. J. Young. |
| " Hochelaga | " | | J. Laporte. |
| " Jacques Cartier | " | | M. F. Valois. |
| Napierville | " | | J. O. Bureau. |
| Niagara, Town | | " | J. C. Morrison. |
| Nicolet | " | | T. Fortier. |
| Norfolk | | " | Hon. J. Rolph. |
| Northumberland, E. R. | | " | Jas. Ross. |
| " W. R. | | " | S. Smith. |
| Ontario, N. R. | | " | I. Gould. |
| " S. R. | | " | J. M. Lumsden. |
| Ottawa, County | " | | A. Cooke. |
| Oxford, N. R. | | " | D. Matheson. |
| " S. R. | | " | Hon. F. Hincks. |
| " " | | " | E. Cook. |
| Peel | | " | J. C. Aikins. |
| Perth | | " | T. M. Daly. |
| Peterborough | | " | J. Langton. |
| " | | " | W. S. Conger. |
| Pontiac | " | | J. Egan. |
| Portneuf | " | | J. E. Thibaudeau. |
| Prescott | | " | H. W. McCann. |
| Prince Edward | | " | D. B. Stevenson. |
| Quebec, City | " | | J. Blanchet. |
| " | " | | Cha. Alleyn. |
| " | " | | Hon. J. Chabot. |
| " | " | | G. H. Simard. |
| " | " | | G. O. Stuart. |
| Quebec, County | " | | P. J. O. Chauveau. |
| " | " | | F. Evanturel. |
| Renfrew | | " | Hon. F. Hincks. |
| " | | " | J. Supple. |
| Rimouski | " | | J. C. Taché. |
| " | " | | M. G. Baby. |
| Richelieu | " | | J. B. Guevremont |

## Legislative Assembly—(Continued.)

| Constituencies. | L. C. | U. C. | Members. |
|---|---|---|---|
| Rouville | " | | J. N. Poulin. |
| " | " | | W. H. Chaffers. |
| Russell | | " | G. B. Lyon. |
| Saguenay | " | | P. G. Huot. |
| St. Hyacinthe | " | | L. V. Sicotte. |
| St. Johns | " | | F. Bourassa. |
| St. Maurice | " | | L. L. Desaulniers. |
| Shefford | " | | Hon. L. T. Drummond. |
| Sherbrooke, Town | " | | A. T. Galt. |
| Sherbrooke and Wolfe | " | | W. L. Felton. |
| Simcoe, N. R. | | " | A. Morrison. |
| Simcoe, S. R. | | " | W. B. Robinson. |
| Stanstead | " | | T. L. Terrill. |
| Soulanges | " | | L. H. Masson. |
| Stormont | | " | W. Mattice. |
| Temiscouata | " | | B. Dionne. |
| Terrebonne | " | | G. M. Prevost. |
| " | " | | L. S. Morin. |
| Three Rivers, Town | " | | A. Polette. |
| Toronto, City | | " | Hon. J. H. Cameron. |
| " | | " | J. G. Bowes. |
| Two Mountains | " | | J. B. Daoust. |
| Vaudreuil | " | | J. B. Mongenais. |
| Verchères | " | | G. E. Cartier. |
| Victoria | | " | Jas. Smith. |
| Waterloo, N. R. | | " | M. H. Foley. |
| " S. R. | | " | R. Ferrie. |
| Welland | | " | J. Frazer. |
| Wellington, N. R. | | " | W. Clarke. |
| " S. R. | | " | A. J. Fergusson. |
| Wentworth, N. R. | | " | R. Spence. |
| " S. R. | | " | S. B. Freeman. |
| Yamaska | " | | Ignace Gill. |
| York, N. R. | | " | J. Hartman. |
| " E. R. | | " | Amos Wright. |
| " W. R. | | " | J. W. Gamble. |

# SIXTH PARLIAMENT.

13th January, 1858, to 10th June, 1861.

130 Members—65 for each section of the Province.

| Constituencies. | L. C. | U. C. | Members. |
|---|---|---|---|
| Argenteuil.................... | " | | S. Bellingham. |
| " ..................... | " | | J. J. C. Abbott. |
| Bagot...................... | " | | M. Laframboise. |
| Beauce .................... | " | | D. Ross. |
| Beauharnois............... | " | | G. Ouimet. |
| Bellechasse............... | " | | O. C. Fortier. |
| Berthier ................. | " | | E. U. Piché. |
| Bonaventure............... | " | | J. Meagher. |
| Brant, E. R................ | | " | D. Christie. |
| " .................... | | " | H. Finlayson. |
| " W. R............... | | " | H. Biggar. |
| Brockville, Town........... | | " | G. Sherwood. |
| Brome..................... | " | | J. M. Ferres. |
| Carleton ................. | | " | W. F. Powell. |
| Chambly.................... | " | | L. Lacoste. |
| Champlain ................ | " | | J. E. Turcotte. |
| Charlevoix................ | " | | C. Cimon. |
| Chateauguay............... | " | | H. Starnes. |
| Chicoutimi and Saguenay....... | " | | D. E. Price. |
| Compton .................. | " | | J. H. Pope. |
| Cornwall, Town............ | | " | Hon. J. S. Macdonald. |
| Dorchester ............... | " | | H. L. Langevin. |
| Drummond and Arthabaska..... | • | | C. Dunkin. |
| Dundas.................... | | " | J. W. Cook. |
| Durham, E. R.............. | | " | F. H. Burton. |
| " W. R............... | | " | H. Munro. |
| Elgin, E. R............... | | " | L. Burwell. |
| " W. R............... | | " | G. Macbeth. |
| Essex ...................... | | " | J. MacLeod. |
| Frontenac................. | | " | H. Smith. |
| Gaspé .................... | • | | J. LeBoutillier. |
| Glengarry................. | | " | D. A. Macdonald. |
| Grenville, S. R........... | | " | W. Patrick. |
| Grey ..................... | | " | J. S. Hogan. |
| Grey..................... | | " | J. T. Purdy. |
| Haldimand ................ | | " | W. L. Mackenzie. |
| " ...................... | | " | M. Harcourt. |
| Halton.................... | | " | J. White. |
| Hamilton, City............ | | " | I. Buchanan. |

7

## Legislative Assembly—(*Continued.*)

| Constituencies. | L. C. | U. C. | Members. |
|---|---|---|---|
| Hastings, N. R. | | " | G. Benjamin. |
| "   S. R. | | " | L. Wallbridge. |
| Hochelaga | " | | J. Laporte. |
| Huntingdon | " | | R. B. Somerville. |
| Huron and Bruce | | " | J. Holmes. |
| Iberville | " | | C. J. Laberge. |
| Jacques Cartier | " | | T. Z. Tassé. |
| Joliette | " | | J. H. Jobin. |
| Kamouraska | " | | J. C. Chapais. |
| Kent | | " | A. McKellar. |
| Kingston, City | | " | Hon. J. A. Macdonald. |
| Lambton | | " | Hon. M. Cameron. |
| " | | " | H. F. Mackenzie. |
| Lanark, N. R. | | " | R. Bell. |
| "   S. R. | | " | A. W. Playfair. |
| Laprairie | " | | Hon. T. J. J. Loranger. |
| L'Assomption | " | | L. Archambault. |
| Laval | " | | P. Labelle. |
| Lennox and Addington | | " | D. Roblin. |
| Leeds and Grenville, N. R. | | " | B. R. Church. |
| "      " | | " | O. R. Gowan. |
| "      S. R. | | " | B. Tett. |
| Lincoln | | " | Hon. W. H. Merritt. |
| " | | " | J. C. Rykert. |
| L'Islet | " | | L. B. Caron. |
| " | " | | C. F. Fournier. |
| Levis | " | | Hon. F. Lemieux. |
| London, City | | " | J. Carling. |
| Lotbinière | " | | J. O'Farrell. |
| " | " | | Hon. L. T. Drummond. |
| Maskinongé | " | | L. H. Gauvreau. |
| " | " | | Geo. Caron. |
| Megantic | " | | N. Hébert. |
| Middlesex, E. R. | | " | M. Talbot. |
| "   " | | " | R. Craik. |
| "   W. R. | | " | J. Scatcherd. |
| "   " | | " | A. P. Macdonald. |
| Missisquoi | " | | H. H. Whitney. |
| Montcalm | " | | J. Dufresne. |
| Montmagny | " | | J. O. Beaubien |
| Montmorenci | " | | Hon. J. Cauchon. |
| Montreal City | " | | A. A. Dorion. |
| " | " | | J. Rose. |
| " | " | | T. D. McGee. |
| Napierville | " | | J. O. Bureau. |
| Niagara, Town | | " | J. Simpson. |
| Nicolet | " | | J. Gaudet. |

## Legislative Assembly—(Continued.)

| Constituencies. | L. C. | U. C. | Members. |
|---|---|---|---|
| Norfork............................ | | " | W. Powell. |
| Northumberland, E. R.......... | | " | J. B. Clarke. |
| Northumberland, W. R.......... | | " | Sidney Smith. |
| Ontario, N. R..................... | | " | I. Gould. |
| Ontario, S. R..................... | | " | O. Mowat. |
| Ottawa, City...................... | | " | R. W. Scott. |
| Ottawa, County.................. | " | | D. E. Papineau |
| Oxford, N. R..................... | | " | G. Brown. |
| " | | " | W. McDougall. |
| Oxford, S. R..................... | | " | S. Connor. |
| Peel.............................. | | " | J. C. Aikins. |
| Perth.............................. | | " | T. M. Daly. |
| Peterborough .................... | | " | T. Short. |
| Pontiac .......................... | " | | E. Heath. |
| Portneuf.......................... | " | | J. E. Thibaudeau. |
| Prescott.......................... | | " | H. W. McCann. |
| Prince Edward.................... | | " | W. C. Dorland. |
| Quebec, City..................... | " | | Hon. C. Alleyn. |
| " | " | | G. H. Simard. |
| " | " | | H. Dubord. |
| Quebec, (East)................... | " | | P. G. Huot. |
| Quebec, County.................. | " | | Chs. Panet. |
| Renfrew........................... | | " | J. L. McDougald. |
| " | | " | Hon. W. Cayley. |
| Richmond and Wolfe............ | " | | W. H. Webb. |
| Richelieu.......................... | " | | J. F. Sincennes. |
| Rimouski.......................... | " | | M. G. Baby. |
| Rouville .......................... | " | | T. E. Campbell, C. B. |
| Russell............................ | | " | G. B. L. Fellowes. |
| " | | " | J. W. Loux. |
| St. Hyacinthe.................... | " | | Hon. L. V. Sicotte. |
| St. Johns, Town................. | " | | F. Bourassa. |
| St. Maurice....................... | " | | L. L. Desaulniers. |
| Shefford.......................... | " | | Hon. L. T. Drummond. |
| " | " | | A. B. Foster. |
| Sherbrooke, Town............... | " | | A. T. Galt. |
| Simcoe, N. R..................... | | " | A. Morrison. |
| " S. R..................... | | " | T. R. Ferguson. |
| Soulanges......................... | " | | D. A. Coutlée. |
| Stanstead ........................ | " | | Hon. T. L. Terrill. |
| Stormont.......................... | | " | W. D. Mattice. |
| Temiscouata...................... | " | | B. Dionne. |
| Terrebonne........................ | " | | L. S. Morin. |
| Three Rivers, City............... | " | | W. M. Dawson. |
| Toronto, City..................... | | " | Geo. Brown. |
| " | | " | J. H. Robinson, jr. |

### Legislative Assembly—(*Continued.*)

| Constituencies. | L. C. | U. C. | Members. |
|---|---|---|---|
| Two Mountains.................... | " | | J. B. Daoust. |
| Vaudreuil........................ | " | | Hon. R. U. Harwood. |
| "  .................... | " | | J. B. Mongenais. |
| Verchères........................ | " | | Hon. G. E. Cartier. |
| Victoria......................... | | " | J. Cameron. |
| Waterloo, N. R.................. | | " | M. H. Foley. |
| "  S. R.................. | | " | Wm. Scott. |
| Welland......................... | | " | G. McMicken. |
| Wellington, N. R............... | | " | Chs. Allan. |
| "  "  ................ | | " | Jas. Ross. |
| "  S. R............... | | " | D. Stirton. |
| Wentworth, N. R.............. | | " | W. Notman. |
| "  S. R.............. | | " | J. Rymal. |
| Yamaska........................ | " | | Ignace Gill. |
| York, N. R..................... | | " | J. Hartman. |
| "  "  ................ | | " | A. Wilson. |
| "  E. R................. | | " | Amos Wright. |
| "  W. R................ | | " | W. P. Howland. |

## SEVENTH PARLIAMENT.

15th *July*, 1861, *to* 16th *May*, 1863.

**130 Members—65 for each section of the Province.**

| Constituencies. | L. C. | U. C. | Members. |
|---|---|---|---|
| Argenteuil........................ | " | | J. J. C. Abbott. |
| Bagot............................ | " | | M. Laframboise. |
| Beauce........................... | " | | H. E. Taschereau. |
| Beauharnois...................... | " | | P. Denis. |
| Bellechasse....................... | " | | E. Rémillard. |
| Berthier.......................... | " | | P. E. Dostaler. |
| Bonaventure...................... | " | | T. Robitaille. |
| Brant, E. R...................... | | " | J. Y. Bown. |
| Brant, W. R..................... | | " | W. Ryerson. |
| Brockville, Town................. | | " | Hon. G. Sherwood. |
| Brome........................... | " | | M. Sweet. |
| "  .................... | " | | C. Dunkin. |
| Carleton ........................ | | " | W. F. Powell. |
| Chambly......................... | " | | C. Boucher de Boucherville. |
| Champlain....................... | " | | J. J. Ross. |
| Charlevoix....................... | " | | A. Gagnon. |

## Legislative Assembly—(Continued.)

| Constituencies. | L. C. | U. C. | Members. |
|---|---|---|---|
| Chateaugai | " | | H. Starnes. |
| Chicoutimi & Saguenay | " | | D. E. Price. |
| Compton | " | | J. H. Pope. |
| Cornwall, Town | | " | Hon. J. S. Macdonald. |
| Dorchester | " | | H. L. Langevin. |
| Drummond & Arthabaska | " | | J. B. E. Dorion. |
| Dundas | | " | J. S. Ross. |
| Durham, E. R. | | " | J. S. Smith. |
| " W. R. | | " | H. Munro. |
| Elgin, E. R. | | " | L. Burwell. |
| " W. R. | | " | G. Macbeth. |
| " | | " | J. Scoble. |
| Essex | | " | A. Rankin. |
| " | | " | J. O'Connor. |
| Frontenac | | " | J. Morton. |
| Gaspé | " | | J. LeBoutillier. |
| Glengarry | | " | D. A. Macdonald. |
| Grenville, S. R. | | " | W. Patrick. |
| Grey | | " | G. Jackson. |
| Haldimand | | " | M. Harcourt. |
| Halton | | " | J. White. |
| Hamilton, City | | " | I. Buchanan. |
| Hastings, N. R. | | " | G. Benjamin. |
| " S. R. | | " | L. Wallbridge. |
| Hochelaga | " | | J. P. Falkner. |
| " | " | | Hon. A. A. Dorion. |
| Huntingdon | " | | R. B. Somerville. |
| Huron & Bruce | | " | J. Dickson. |
| Iberville | " | | A. Dufresne. |
| Jacques Cartier | " | | T. Z. Tané. |
| Joliette | " | | J. H. Jobin. |
| Kamouraska | " | | J. C. Chapais. |
| Kent | | " | A. McKellar. |
| Kingston, City | | " | Hon. J. A. Macdonald. |
| Lambton | | " | A. Mackenzie. |
| Lanark, N. R. | | " | R. Bell. |
| Lanark, S. R. | | " | A. Morris. |
| Lapraire | " | | Hon. T. J. J. Loranger. |
| " | " | | A. Pinsonneault. |
| L'Assomption | " | | A. Archambault. |
| Laval | " | | P. Labelle. |
| " | " | | Hon. L. S. Morin. |
| Leeds and Grenville, N. R. | | " | F. Jones. |
| Leeds, S. R. | | " | B. Tett. |
| Lennox and Addington | | " | A. F. Hooper. |
| Levis | " | | J. G. Blanchet. |
| Lincoln | | " | J. C. Rykert. |

## Legislative Assembly—(*Continued.*)

| Constituencies. | L. C. | U. C. | Members. |
|---|---|---|---|
| L'Islet............................ | " | | C. F. Fournier. |
| London, City..................... | | " | J. Carling. |
| Litbinière........................ | " | | H. G. Joly. |
| Maskinongé...................... | " | | G. Caron. |
| Megantic......................... | " | | N. Hébert. |
| Middlesex, E. R................. | | " | Hon. M. P. Portman. |
|    "     W. R................. | | " | T. Scatcherd. |
| Missisquoi........................ | " | | J. O'Halloran. |
| Montcalm......................... | " | | J. L. Martin. |
|    "  ............................ | " | | J. Dufresne. |
| Montmagny....................... | " | | J. O. Beaubien. |
| Montmorenci...................... | " | | Hon. J. Cauchon. |
| Montreal, City, (West).......... | " | | T. D. McGee. |
|    "     (Centre)......... | " | | Hon. J. Rose. |
|    "     (East).......... | " | | Hon. G. E. Cartier. |
| Napierville....................... | " | | J. O. Bureau. |
|    "  ............................ | " | | P. Benoit. |
| Niagara, Town.................... | | " | J. Simpson. |
| Nicolet........................... | " | | J. Gaudet |
| Norfolk........................... | | " | A. Walsh. |
| Northumberland, E. R........... | | " | J. L. Biggar. |
|    "     W. R........... | | " | J. Cockburn. |
| Ontario, N. R.................... | | " | M. C. Cameron, |
|    "     S. R.................... | | " | Hon. O. Mowat. |
| Ottawa, City..................... | | " | R. W. Scott. |
|    "     County................... | " | | W. M. Dawson. |
| Oxford, N. R..................... | | " | W. McDougall. |
|    "     S. R..................... | | " | S. Connor. |
|    "     "  ........................ | | " | Hon. Geo. Brown. |
| Peel.............................. | | " | Hon. J. H. Cameron. |
| Perth............................. | | " | Hon. M. H. Foley. |
|    "  ............................ | | " | T. M. Daly. |
| Peterborough..................... | | " | F. W. Haultain. |
| Pontiac........................... | " | | J. Poupore. |
| Portneuf.......................... | " | | J. D. Brousseau. |
| Prescott.......................... | | " | H. W. McCann. |
| Prince Edward.................... | | " | W. Anderson. |
| Quebec, City, (East)............. | " | | P. G. Huot. |
| Quebec, City, (Centre).......... | " | | G. H. Simard. |
| Quebec, City, (West)............ | " | | Hon. C. Alleyn. |
| Quebec, County.................. | " | | F. Evanturel. |
| Renfrew.......................... | | " | D. McLachlin. |
| Richmond and Wolfe............ | " | | C. DeCazes. |
| Richelieu......................... | " | | J. Beaudreau. |
| Rimouski......................... | " | | G. Sylvain. |
| Rouville.......................... | " | | Hon. L. T. Drummond. |
| Russell........................... | | " | R. Bell. |

## Legislative Assembly—(Continued.)

| Constituencies. | L. C. | U. C. | Members. |
|---|---|---|---|
| St. Hyacinthe | " | | Hon. L. V. Sicotte. |
| St. Johns | " | | F. Bourassa. |
| St. Maurice | " | | L. L. Desaulniers. |
| Shefford | " | | L. S. Huntington. |
| Sherbrooke, Town | " | | Hon. A. T. Galt. |
| Simcoe, N. R. | | " | A. Morison. |
| Simcoe, S. R. | | " | T. R. Ferguson. |
| Soulanges | " | | J. B. J. Prevost. |
| Stanstead | " | | A. Knight. |
| Stormont | | " | S. Ault. |
| Temiscouata | " | | M. W. Baby. |
| Terrebonne | " | | L. Labreche Viger. |
| Three Rivers, City | " | | J. E. Turcotte. |
| Toronto, City, (West) | | " | J. B. Robinson. |
| Toronto, City, East | | " | J. Crawford. |
| Two Mountains | " | | J. B. Daoust. |
| Vaudreuil | " | | J. B. Mongenais. |
| Verchères | " | | A. E. Kierskowski. |
| " | " | | C. F. Panchaud. |
| Victoria | | " | J. W. Dunsford. |
| Waterloo, N. R. | | " | Hon. M. H. Foley. |
| Waterloo, S. R. | | " | J. Cowan. |
| Welland | | " | T. C. Street. |
| Wellington, N. R. | | " | W. Clarke. |
| Wellington, S. R. | | " | D. Stirton. |
| Wentworth, N. R. | | " | W. Notman. |
| Wentworth, S. R. | | " | Jos. Rymal. |
| Yamaska | " | | M. Fortin. |
| York, N. R. | | " | A. Wilson. |
| York, E. R. | | " | Amos Wright. |
| York, W. R. | | " | W. P. Howland. |

# EIGHTH PARLIAMENT.

3rd July, 1863, to————

130 Members—65 for each section of the Province.

## Legislative Assembly—(*Continued.*)

| Constituencies. | L. C. | U. C. | Members. |
|---|---|---|---|
| Beauharnois | " | | P. Denis. |
| Bellechasse | " | | E. Rémillard. |
| Berthier | " | | A. H. Paquette. |
| Bonaventure | " | | T. Robitaille. |
| Brant, E. R. | | " | J. Y. Bown. |
| Brant, W. R. | | " | E. B. Wood. |
| Brockville, Town | | " | F. H. Chambers. |
| Brome | " | | C. Dunkin. |
| Carleton | | " | W. F. Powell. |
| Chambly | " | | C. Boucher de Boucherville. |
| Champlain | " | | J. J. Ross. |
| Charlevoix | " | | A. Gagnon. |
| Chauteaugai | " | | Hon. L. H. Holton. |
| Chicoutimi and Saguenay | " | | D. E. Price. |
| " | " | | P. A. Tremblay. |
| Compton | " | | J. H. Pope. |
| Cornwall, Town | | " | Hon. J. S. Macdonald. |
| Dorchester | " | | H. L. Langevin. |
| Drummond and Arthabaska | " | | J. B. E. Dorion. |
| Dundas | | " | J. S. Ross. |
| Durham, E. R. | | " | J. S. Smith. |
| Durham, W. R. | | " | H. Munro. |
| Elgin, E. R. | | " | L. Burwell. |
| Elgin, W. R. | | " | J. Scoble. |
| Essex | | " | A. Rankin. |
| Frontenac | | " | W. Ferguson. |
| Gaspé | " | | J. LeBoutillier. |
| Glengarry | | " | D. A. Macdonald. |
| Grenville, S. R. | | " | W. Shanly. |
| Grey | | " | G. Jackson. |
| Haldimand | | " | D. Thompson. |
| Halton | | " | J. White. |
| Hamilton, City | | " | Hon. I. Buchanan. |
| " | | " | C. Magill. |
| Hastings, N. R. | | " | T. C. Wallbridge. |
| Hastings, S. R. | | " | Hon. L. Wallbridge. |
| Hochelaga | " | | Hon. A. A. Dorion. |
| Huntingdon | " | | R. B. Somerville. |
| Huron and Bruce | | " | J. Dickson. |
| Iberville | " | | A. Dufresne. |
| Jacques Cartier | " | | T. Z. Tassé. |
| " | " | | G. G. Gaucher. |
| Joliette | " | | H. Cornellier dit Grandchamps. |
| Kamouraska | " | | J. C. Chapais. |
| Kent | | " | A. McKellar. |
| Kingston City | | " | Hon. J. A Macdonald. |
| Lambton | | " | A. Mackenzie. |

## Legislative Assembly—(Continued.)

| Constituencies. | L. C. | U. C. | Members. |
|---|---|---|---|
| Lanark, N. R. | | " | R. Bell. |
| "    "         | | " | Hon. W. MacDougall. |
| "    S. R.     | | " | A. Morris. |
| Laprairie       | " | | A. Pinsonneault. |
| L'Assomption    | " | | L. Archambault. |
| Laval           | " | | J. H. Bellerose. |
| Leeds and Grenville, N. R. | | " | F. Jones. |
| Leeds, S. R.    | | " | A. N. Richards. |
| "    "          | | " | D. F. Jones. |
| Lennox and Addington | | " | R. J. Cartwright. |
| Levis           | " | | J. G. Blanchet. |
| Lincoln         | | " | W. McGiverin. |
| L'Islet         | " | | L. B. Caron. |
| London, City    | | " | Hon. J. Carling. |
| Lotbinière      | " | | H. G. Joly. |
| Maskinongé      | " | | M. Houde. |
| Megantic        | " | | G. Irvine. |
| Middlesex, E. R. | | " | C. Wilson. |
| "    W. R.      | | " | T. Scatcherd. |
| Missisquoi      | " | | J. O'Halloran. |
| Montcalm        | " | | J. Dufresne. |
| Montmagny       | " | | J. O. Beaubien. |
| Montmorenci     | " | | Hon. J. Cauchon. |
| Montreal City, (West) | " | | Hon. T. D. McGee. |
| "    (Centre)   | " | | Hon. J. Rose. |
| "    (East)     | " | | Hon. G. E. Cartier. |
| Napierville     | " | | S. Cartal dit Larose. |
| Niagara, Town.  | | " | J. Simpson. |
| "    "          | | " | A. Morrison. |
| Nicolet         | " | | J. Gaudet. |
| Norfolk         | | " | A. Walsh. |
| Northumberland, E. R. | | " | J. L. Biggar. |
| "    W. R.      | | " | J. Cockburn. |
| Ontario, N. R.  | | " | Hon. W. McDougall. |
| "    "          | | " | M. C. Cameron. |
| "    S. R.      | | " | Hon. O. Mowat. |
| "    "          | | " | T. N. Gibbs. |
| Ottawa, City    | | " | J. M. Currier. |
| "    County     | " | | Alonzo Wright. |
| Oxford, N. R.   | | " | H. F. Mackenzie. |
| "    S. R.      | | " | Hon. Geo. Brown. |
| Peel            | | " | Hon. J. H. Cameron. |
| Perth           | | " | T. Mayfarlane. |
| Peterborough    | | " | W. S. Conger. |
| "    "          | | " | T. W. Haultain. |
| Pontiac         | " | | J. Poupore. |
| Portneuf        | " | | J. D. Brousseau. |

| Constituencies. | L. C. | U. C. | Members. |
|---|---|---|---|
| Prescott | | " | T. Higginson. |
| Prince Edward | | " | W. Ross. |
| Quebec City, (East) | " | | P. G. Huot. |
| " (Centre) | " | | Hon. I. Thibaudeau. |
| " (West) | " | | Hon. Chs. Alleyn. |
| Quebec, County | " | | Hon. F. Evanturel. |
| Renfrew | | " | R. McIntyre. |
| Richmond and Wolfe | " | | W. H. Webb. |
| Richelieu | " | | J. F. Perreault. |
| Rimouski | " | | G. Sylvain. |
| Rouville | " | | J. N. Poulin. |
| Russell | | " | R. Bell. |
| St. Hyacinthe | " | | Hon. L. V. Sicotte. |
| " | " | | R. Raymond. |
| St. Johns | " | | F. Bourassa. |
| St. Maurice | " | | C. Lajoie. |
| Shefford | " | | Hon. L. S. Huntington. |
| Sherbrooke, Town | " | | Hon. A. T. Galt. |
| Simcoe, N. R. | | " | T. D. McConkey. |
| " S. R. | | " | T. R. Ferguson. |
| Soulanges | " | | W. Duckett. |
| Stanstead | " | | A. Knight. |
| Stormont | | " | S. Ault. |
| Temiscouata | " | | J. B. Pouliot. |
| Terrebonne | " | | L. Labrèche-Viger. |
| Three Rivers, Town | " | | Hon. J. E. Turcotte. |
| " | " | | C. Boucher de Niverville. |
| Toronto City, (West) | | " | J. McDonald. |
| " (East) | | " | A. M. Smith. |
| Two Mountains | " | | J. B. Daoust. |
| Vaudreuil | " | | A. C. D. Harwood. |
| Verchères | " | | F. Geoffrion. |
| Victoria | | " | J. W. Dunsford. |
| Waterloo, N. R. | | " | Hon. M. H. Foley. |
| " " | | " | J. E. Bowman. |
| " S. R. | | " | J. Cowan. |
| Welland | | " | T. C. Street. |
| Wellington, N. R. | | " | T. S. Parker. |
| " S. R. | | " | D. Stirton. |
| Wentworth, N. R. | | " | W. Notman. |
| " " | | " | J. McMonies. |
| " S. R. | | " | J. Rymal. |
| Yamaska | " | | M. Fortier. |
| York, N. R. | | " | J. P. Wells. |
| " E. R. | | " | Amos Wright. |
| " W. R. | | " | Hon. W. P. Howland. |

## Contested Elections, Special Elections, Resignations and Deaths of Elected Members of Legislative Council.

### 1856 to 1865.

Armand, Hon. Jos. F., Alma Division, reported duly elected, 23rd April, 1860.

Baby, Hon. F., Stadacona, elected on 17th June, 1851, in the room of F. G. Huot ; reported duly elected, 16th March, 1863, died in 1864.

Blair, Hon. A. J. Ferguson, Brock, re-elected on 28th March, 1863, after his appointment as Receiver General.

Bossé, Hon. J. N., La Durantaye, elected on 29th June, 1864, in the room of Hon. F. Lemieux, deceased.

Bureau, Hon. J. O., De Lorimier, re-elected on 76th February, 1862, after his appointment as Provincial Secretary and Registrar.

Burnham, Hon. A. A., Newcastle, was elected on 17th September, 1863, in the room of Hon. A. Jeffrey, deceased.

Cameron, Hon. M., St. Clair, vacated his seat by appointment as Queen's Printer, on 25th April, 1863.

Campbell, Hon., A. Cataraqui, re-elected on 30th April, 1864, after his appointment as Commissioner of Crown Lands.

Chaffers, Hon. W. H., Rougemont, was elected on 8th January, 1864, in the room of Hon. L. A. Dessaulles, appointed Clerk of the Crown and Peace, Montreal.

Currie, Hon. J. G., Niagara, was elected on 4th September, 1862, in the room of Hon. W. H. Merritt, deceased.

Dessaulles, Hon. L. A., Rougemont, vacated his seat on being appointed Clerk of the Crown and Peace, Montreal, in December, 1863.

Flint Hon. B., Trent, was elected on 21st July, 1863, in the room of Hon. Sidney Smith, resigned.

Gingras, Hon. J. E., Stadacona, was elected on 19th September, 1864, in the room of Hon. F. Baby, deceased.

Guèvremont, Hon. J. B., Sorel, declared not duly elected for want of the required qualification, 30th April, 1860 ; re-elected, 18th June, 1860.

Harwood, Hon. R. U., Rigaud, died in May, 1863.

Holton, Hon. L. H., Victoria, vacated his seat on being appointed Minister of Finance, on 16th May, 1863 ; Hon. T. Ryan, was elected in his room ; Mr. Holton elected for Chateauguay.

Huot, Hon. F. G., Stadacona, his election declared void, 18th April, 1861.

Jeffrey, Hon. A., Newcastle, died on 27th July, 1863 ; Hon. A. A. Burnham, elected in his room.

Kierskowski, Hon. A. E., Montarville, declared not duly elected for the want of the required qualification, 18th April, 1861.

Lacoste, Hon. L., Montarville, was elected on 17th June, 1861, in the room of Hon. A. E. Kierskowski.

Letellier de St. Just, Hon. L., Grandville, re-elected on 5th June, 1863, after his appointment as Minister of Agriculture.

Merritt, Hon. W. H., Niagara, died on 5th July, 1862.

Murney, Hon. E., Trent, died in August, 1861.

McCrea, Hon. W., Western, was elected on 18th September, 1862, in the room of Hon. Sir A. N. MacNab, deceased, Mr. McCrea appointed County Judge, Brant, in December, 1865.

McMurrich, Hon. J., Saugeen, elected 9th May, 1862, in the room of the Hon. J. Patton, who vacated his seat by his appointment as Solicitor General, U. C.

MacNab, Hon. Sir A. N., Western, was elected on 24th November, 1860, in the room of Hon. J. Prince, appointed Judge ; died on 8th August, 1862.

Olivier, Hon. L. A., De Lanaudière, was elected on 6th April, 1863, in the room of Hon. A. R. Lajoie, deceased.

Patton, Hon. J., Saugeen, vacated his seat on being appointed Solicitor General for U. C., Hon. J. McMurrich was elected in his room.

Prince, Hon. J., Western, vacated his seat by his appointment as Judge, District of Algoma

## Contested Elections, Special Elections, &c.—(*Continued.*)

Prudhomme, Hon. E., Rigaud, was elected on 3rd June, 1863, in the room of Hon. R. U Harwood, deceased.

Ryan, Hon. Tho., Victoria, was elected on 19th June, 1863, in the room of Hon. L. H. Holton, who vacated his seat, having been appointed Minister of Finance.

Sanborn, Hon. J. S., Wellington, was elected on 8th May, 1863, in the room of Hon. Hollis Smith, deceased.

Skead, Hon. J., Rideau, was elected on 21st April, 1862, in the room of Hon. P. M. Vankoughnet, appointed Chancellor, U. C.

Smith, Hon. Hollis, Wellington, his disease reported 9th April, 1863.

Smith, Sidney, Trent, was elected on 26th September, 1861, in the room of Hon. E. Murney, deceased, Mr. Smith resigned in 1863.

Tessier, Hon. J. U., Gulf, re-elected on 23rd June, 1863, after his appointment as Commissioner of Public Works.

Vidal, Hon. A., St. Clair, was elected on 19th September, 1863, in the room of Hon. J. Wilson, appointed Judge.

Wilson, Hon. J., St. Clair, was elected on 16th May, 1863, in the room of the Hon. M. Cameron, appointed Queen's Printer; vacated his seat on being appointed Puisne Judge of Court of Common Pleas, U. C. on 22nd July, 1863.

## Contested Elections, Special Elections, Resignations and Demise of Members of the Legislative Assembly.

## 1841 to 1865.

## FIRST PARLIAMENT.

### 8th April, 1841, to 23rd September, 1844.

Aylwin, Hon. T. C., Portneuf, having vacated his seat on being appointed Solicitor General for Lower Canada, on 24th September, 1842, was re-elected on 20th October, 1842.

Baldwin, Hon. R., Hastings and 4th Riding of York, elected to serve for Hastings, on 25th August, 1841. Vacated his seat on being appointed Attorney General for U. C., on 16th September, 1842. Writ for new Election issued. Special return made, 17th October, 1842. Mr. Baldwin elected for Rimouski, 30th January, 1843.

Beaubien, P., Montreal City, elected on 22nd November, 1843, in the room of Hon. G. Moffatt, resigned.

Borne, M., Rimouski, resigned on 15th December, 1842.

Boulton, H. J., Niagara Town, declared the Member for that Town, 26th September, 1842.

Buchanan, I., Toronto, City, resigned on 2nd January, 1843.

Burnet, D., Quebec City, resigned on 26th August, 1843.

Campbell, E. C., Niagara Town. His Election declared null and void, 26th Sept., 1842.

Chabot, J., Quebec City, elected on 18th September, 1843, in the room of D. Burnet.

Day, C. D., Ottawa, County, appointed Judge on 21st June, 1842.

Delisle, A. M., Montreal, County, vacated his seat on 13th July, 1843, by being appointed Clerk of the Crown.

DeSalaberry, M. A., Rouville, vacated his seat, being appointed Registrar, Richelieu District, 1st January, 1842.

Desrivieres, H., Vercheres, resigned on 6th November, 1841.

DeWitt, J., Leinster, elected on 8th August, 1842.

Draper, W. H., Russell, appointed Member of Legislative Council, on 10th April, 1843.

Duggan, G., York, 2nd Riding. His election declared null and void, 26th September, 1842. Is re-elected 22nd November, 1842.

## Contested Elections, Special Elections, &c.—(Continued.)

Dunlop, W., Huron. His name substituted for that of J. M. Strachan, 23th August, 1841.

Dunscomb, J. W., Beauharnois, resigned 13th July, 1842, he being appointed Warden, Trinity House, Montreal.

Franchère, T., Rouville, elected 25th September, 1843.

Forbes, C. J., Two Mountains, elected on 18th April, 1842.

Gilchrist, J., Northumberland, N. R., will not returned.

Harrison, Hon. S. B., Kingston, elected on 1st July, 1841

Hincks, F., Oxford, resigned on 3rd June, 1841, was re-elected on 6th July, 1842

Jobin, A., Montreal County, was elected on 28th October, 1843.

Judah, H., Champlain, was elected on 22nd September, 1843.

Killaly, H. H., London Town, vacates his seat on 21st December, 1841, being appointed Chairman of Board of Works. He is re-elected on 28th September, 1842, resigns his seat 30th November, 1843.

Kimber, R. J., Champlain, was appointed member of the Legislative Council on 4th September, 1843.

Lacoste, L., Chambly, was elected on 22nd October, 1843, in room of J. Yule, resigned.

LaFontaine, L. H., York, 4th Riding, elected on 21st September, 1841. Vacated his seat on 18th September, 1842, being appointed Attorney-General for L. C., was re-elected on 8th October, 1842

Leslie, J., Verchères, was elected on 28th December, 1841

Manahan, A., Kingston, vacates his seat on 18th June, 1841, being appointed collector of Customs, Toronto.

Moffatt, Hon. G., Montreal City, resigned, 30th October, 1843.

Morin, A. N., Nicolet, vacates his seat, on 1st January, 1842, he being appointed District Judge, Rimouski. Resigned his office as Judge on 7th January, 1842.

Morin, Hon. A. N., Saguenay, was elected on 28th November, 1842.

Murney, E., Hastings, new writ (third) issued 9th October, 1843. Mr. Murney elected 4th November, 1843.

Papineau, D. B., Ottawa County, elected 17th August, 1842, vacates his seat on 3rd September, 1844, on being appointed Commissioner of Crown Lands.

Parent, Et., Saguenay, vacates his seat 14th October, 1842, on being appointed Clerk of Executive Council.

Parke, T., Middlesex, vacates his seat, being appointed Surveyor General. He is re-elected on 10th July, 1841.

Prince, J., Essex, return received after the return day.

Raymond, J. M., Leinster, vacates his seat, being appointed District Registrar of Leinster, on 1st January, 1842.

Robertson, C., Two Mountains, died on or about 3rd February, 1842.

Ruel, A. G., Bellechasse, vacated his seat 1st January, 1842, being appointed Registrar, Rimouski.

Sherwood, Hon. H., Toronto City, elected on 6th March, 1843.

Small, J. E., York, 3rd Riding, appointed Solicitor General for U. C. 28th September, 1842; was re-elected on 15th October, 1842

Stuart, W., Russell, was elected on 14th September, 1843.

Turcotte, J. E., St. Maurice, vacated his seat on 6th December, 1841, by his appointment as translator of the laws; was re-elected on 8th July, 1841

Turgeon, A., Bellechasse, was elected on 6th June, 1842

Viger, L. M., Nicolet, was elected on 15th February, 1842.

Viger, Hon. D. B., Richelieu, was appointed President of the Executive Council, on 12th December, 1843.

Wakefield, E. G., Beauharnois, was elected on 9th November, 1842, in room of J. W. Dunscomb resigned.

Walker, Wm., Rouville, was elected on 7th July, 1842, in room of M. A. DeSalaberry appointed registrar, Mr. Walker resigned his seat on 28th August, 1843.

Woods, J., Kent, was declared duly elected, 17th June, 1841.

Yule, J., Chambly, resigned on 22nd September, 1843.

## Contested Elections, Special Elections, &c.—(*Continued.*)

## SECOND PARLIAMENT.

*From* 12th *November*, 1844, *to* 6th *December*, 1847.

Badgley, Hon. W., Missisquoi, was elected on 10th June, 1847, in room of Hon. J. Smith, appointed Judge.

Baldwin, Hon. R., York, 4th Riding, the writ was received on 14th November, 1844.

Cameron, M., Lanark. His election declared void, 21st January, 1845, he is re-elected 28th February, 1845.

Cameron, J. H., Cornwall, was elected on 17th August, 1846.

Cayley, Hon. W., Huron, was elected on 28th February, 1846.

Conger, R. B., Prince Edward, was elected on 1st July, 1846.

DeBleury, C. C. S., Montreal City, died on 15th September, 1862.

Draper, Hon. W. H., London, Town, was elected on 13th February, 1845; resigned on 2nd June, 1847.

Dunlop, Wm., Huron, resigned.

Fournier, C. F., L'Islet, was elected on 6th May, 1847.

Grieve, E., Three Rivers, Town, died on ———. Hon. D. B. Viger, was elected in his room on 14th July, 1845.

Harrison, Hon. S. B., Kent, was appointed Judge of Surrogate Court, on 4th January, 1845.

Johnston, James, Carleton, resigned on 14th May, 1846.

Laterrière, M. P., Saguenay, elected 14th January, 1845.

Lawrason, L., London, Town, resigned on 24th January, 1845.

LeBoutillier, J., Bonaventure, writ received 19th November 1844.

Lemieux, F., Dorchester, was elected on 12th July, 1847.

Lyon, G., Carleton, was elected on 23rd June, 1846.

Munro, G., York, 3rd Riding, declared duly elected 14th March, 1845.

Morin, Hon. A. N., Bellechasse and Saguenay, elected on 13th December, 1844, to serve for Bellechasse.

Macdonald, R., Cornwall, resigned his seat. J. H. Cameron was elected in his room on 17th August, 1846.

Macdonald, J. A., Kingston, appointed Member of Executive Council, on 11th May, 1847; was re-elected on 1st June, 1847.

Nelson, Wm., Richelieu, died in 1863.

Robinson, W. B., Simcoe. Writ received 19th November, 1844. W. B. Robinson appointed Inspector General on 20th December, 1844; re-elected on 13th January, 1845; having resigned as Inspector General on 30th April, 1845, and having been appointed Chief Comr. of Public Works on 22nd June, 1846, he was re-elected on 27th July, 1846.

Roblin, J. P., Prince Edward, was appointed Collector of Customs in May, 1846.

Sherwood, Hon. H., Toronto City, appointed Attorney General for U. C. on 29th May, 1847, was re-elected on 10th June, 1847.

**Small**, Hon. J. E., York, 3rd Riding. His election declared null and void on 14th March, 1845.

Smith, Hon. Jas., Missisquoi, was appointed Judge on 23rd April, 1847.

Taché, E. P., L'Islet, was appointed Deputy Adjutant General of Militia, on 1st July, 1846.

Taschereau, J. A., Dorchester, was elected on 15th September, 1845, in room of P. E. Taschereau, deceased; J. A. Taschereau was appointed Circuit Judge on 22nd May, 1847.

Viger, Hon. D. B., Three Rivers, Town, was elected on 14th July, 1845.

Wilson, J., London, Town, was elected on 3rd July, 1847.

Woods, J., Kent, was elected, **on** 7th February, 1845.

## Contested Elections, Special Elections, &c.—(Continued.)

# THIRD PARLIAMENT.

24th January, 1848, to 6th November, 1851.

Aylwin, Hon. T. C., Quebec, City, appointed Solicitor General for L. C. on 11th March, 1848 ; re-elected 28th March, 1848 ; appointed Judge, Q. B., 28th April, 1848.

Baldwin, Hon. R., York, N. R., appointed Attorney General for U. C., 11th March, 1848 ; re-elected 1st April, 1848.

Beaubien, P., Chambly, appointed Gaol Physician, Montreal, 31st July, 1849.

Blake, W. H., York, E. R., appointed Solicitor General, U. C., 22nd April, 1848 ; re-elected 5th July, 1848 ; appointed Chancellor, U. C., 1st October, 1849.

Brooks, S., Sherbrooke, County, died 22nd March, 1849.

Cameron, M., Kent, declared elected, 2nd March, 1848, appointed Asst. Comr. of Public Works, and Member of the Executive Council, 10th March, 1848 ; re-elected 10th April, 1848, resigned as Member of Executive Council, &c., on 1st February, 1850 ; was re-appointed to Executive Council on 28th October, 1851.

Carmil, P., Oxford. His Election declared null and void, 1st March, 1848. Hon. F. Hincks, declared elected for Oxford, 1st March, 1848.

Cartier, G. E., Verchéres, elected 7th April, 1848.

Chabot, J., Quebec, City, appointed Chief Commissioner of Public Works, 13th December, 1849 ; re-elected 29th January, 1850 ; resigned 31st March, 1850, as Chief Commissioner of Public Works.

Daly, Hon. D., Megantic, appointed to **office** by the Imperial Government.

DeWitt, J., Beauharnois, declared duly elected, 1st March, 1848.

Drummond, L. T., Shefford, appointed Solicitor General, L. C., on 7th June, 1848 ; re-elected 11th July, 1848 ; appointed Attorney General and Member of Executive Council, 28th October, 1851.

Fergusson, A. J., Waterloo, declared duly elected, 8th February, 1849.

Galt, A. T., Sherbrooke, County, elected on 17th April, 1849 ; resigned.

Hincks, Hon. F., Oxford, declared elected, 1st March, 1848 ; appointed Inspector General, 11th March, 1848 ; re-elected on 28th April, 1848.

Hopkins, C., Halton, elected on 15th March, 1850.

Lacoste, L., Chambly, elected on 29th September, 1849.

LaFontaine, Hon. L. H., Montreal, City, and Terrebonne ; appointed Attorney General, L. C., 10th March, 1848 ; re-elected for Montreal, 28th March, 1848.

La Terrière, Hon. M. P., Saguenay, appointed Deputy Adjutant General of Militia, on 8th June, 1848 ; was re-elected on 5th September, 1848.

Leslie, Jas., Verchéres, appointed President of the Executive Council on **11th March,** 1848 ; appointed Member of Legislative Council on 23rd May, 1848.

Letellier, L., Kamouraska, was elected on 1st February, 1851, in room of **F. C. Mougeon,** deceased.

Merritt, W. H., Lincoln, appointed President of Executive Council, 15th September, 1848 ; re-elected 6th October, 1848 ; resigned as President of Executive Council on 7th April, 1850 ; appointed Chief Commissioner of Public Works on 8th April, 1850 ; re-elected 4th May, 1850.

Methot, F. X., Quebec, City, elected 9th June, 1848, in room of Mr. Aylwin.

Macdonald, J. S., Glengarry, appointed Solicitor General, U. C., on 14th December, 1849 ; re-elected on 11th January, 1850.

Mackenzie, W. L., Haldimand, was elected on 21st April, 1851, in room of D. Thompson, deceased.

Perry, P., York, E. R., was elected on 4th December, 1849, died in August, 1851.

Polette, A., Three Rivers, Town, was elected on 26th April, 1851 ; no member having been returned at the General Elections.

Price, J. H., York, S. R., appointed Commissioner of Crown Lands, 11th March, 1848 ; re-elected on 31st March, 1848.

Richards, W. B., Leeds, vacates his seat on 28th October, 1851, being that day appointed Attorney General, U. C.

Ross, D., Megantic, was elected on 1st May, 1850.

Sanborn, J. S., Sherbrooke, County, elected 9th March, 1850.

## Contested Elections, Special Elections, &c.—(*Continued.*)

Viger, Hon. L. M., Terrebonne, elected 14th April, 1848.
Webster, J., Waterloo, his election declared null and void on 8th February, 1849.
Wetenhall, J., Halton, appointed Assistant Commissioner of Public Works, 2nd February, 1850.
Wilson, J., London, Town, resigned his seat, and was re-elected on 21st January, 1850.

## FOURTH PARLIAMENT.

### *24th December, 1851, to 23rd June, 1854.*

Boulton, W. H., Toronto City, his election declared null and void, 29th March, 1853.
Cameron, Hon. M., Huron, appointed President of the Executive Council, on 28th October, 1851, sworn in on 5th March, 1852; re-elected on 12th May, 1852.
Chabot, Hon. J., Bellechasse, appointed Chief Commissioner of Public Works, 23rd September, 1852; re-elected on 4th October, 1852.
Christie, R., Gaspé, declared duly elected 20th August, 1852,
Delong, J., Leeds, elected 13th July, 1853, in room of Hon. W. B. Richards, appointed Judge.
Galt, A. T., Sherbrooke, Town, elected 8th March, 1853, in room of E. Short, appointed Judge.
Hincks, Hon. F., Niagara & Oxford, elects to represent Oxford, 7th September, 1852.
Laterrière, Hon. M. P., Saguenay, Writ returnable on 2nd February, 1852.
Morrison, J. C., Niagara, Town, elected 25th September, 1852; appointed Solicitor General, U. C., 22nd June, 1853; re-elected 13th July, 1853.
Papineau, Hon. L. J., Two Mountains, was elected on 9th July, 1852, in room of W. H. Scott, deceased,
Richards, Hon. W. B., Leeds, appointed Judge on 22nd June, 1853.
Sherwood, Hon. H. Toronto, City, elected 28th April, 1853.
Short, E., Sherbrooke, Town, appointed Judge 12th November, 1852.
Terrill, H. B., Stanstead, died on 28th October, 1852.
Terrill, T. L., Stanstead, elected on 23rd November, 1852.

## FIFTH PARLIAMENT.

### *10th August, 1854, to 28th November, 1857.*

Alleyn, Hon. C., Quebec, City, appointed Member of Executive Council and Chief Commissioner of Public Works, on 26th November, 1857.
Baby, M. G., Rimouski, was elected on 17th Feby, 1857, in room of J. C. Taché, resigned.
Bellingham, S., Argenteuil, his election declared null and void, 29th November, 1854; re-elected 5th January, 1855; second election declared null and void, 3rd April, 1856; is re-elected on 12th May, 1856.
Benjamin, G., Hastings, N. R., was elected on 23rd October, 1856, in room of E. Murney, resigned; died in September, 1864.
Blanchet, J., Quebec, City, resigned 16th March, 1857.
Brodeur, T., Bagot, his election declared null and void, on 13th September, 1854, re-elected on 20th October, 1854.
Cartier, Hon. G. E., Verchères, appointed Provincial Secretary, 27th January, 1855; re-elected, 26th February, 1855.
Cauchon, Hon. J., Montmorency, appointed Commissioner of Crown Lands, 27th January, 1855; re-elected 12th February, 1855,
Cayley, Hon. W., Huron and Bruce, appointed Inspector General, 11th September, 1854; re-elected 4th October, 1854.

## Contested Elections, Special Elections, &c.—(Continued.)

Chabot, Hon. J., Quebec City and Bellechasse, elects to serve for Quebec, 22nd September, 1854, resigned his seat for Quebec, his Election being contested; but no Writ having been issued for a new Election, he retained his seat. (See Australia, 13th February, 1856.)  Appointed Judge of Superior Court, 20th September, 1856.

Chaffers, W. H., Rouville, was elected on 4th October, 1856.

Chapais, J. C., Kamouraska, his election declared null and void, 20th November, 1854; was re-elected on 30th January, 1855.

Chauveau, Hon. P. J. O., Quebec, County, appointed Superintendent of Education, **L. C.,** 1st July, 1855.

Christie, D., Brant, E. R., declared duly elected, 12th March, 1855.

Couger, W. S., Peterborough, was elected on 26th January, 1856, in room of J. Langton, appointed Auditor.

Cook, E., Oxford, S. R., was elected on 9th October, 1854.

Evanturel, F., Quebec, County, was elected on 7th August, 1855, in room of P. J. O. Chauveau.

Fortier, O. C., Bellechasse, was elected on 17th October, 1854, in room of Hon. J. Chabot, elected for Quebec City.

Hincks, Hon. F., Renfrew and Oxford, elects to serve for Renfrew, 18th September, 1854, resigns his seat by letter of 16th November, 1855.

Ham, P. G., Saguenay, writ returnable 1st September, 1854, election declared null and void, 17th November, 1854; re-elected 18th January, 1855.

Langton, J., Peterborough, appointed Auditor of Public Accounts on 27th December, 1855.

LeBoutillier, J., Gaspé, writ returnable 1st September, 1854.

Lemieux, Hon. F., Levis, appointed Chief Commissioner of Public Works, 27th January, 1855; re-elected 10th February, 1855.

Loranger, Hon. T. J. J., Laprairie, appointed Provincial Secretary, 26th November, 1857.

Morin, Hon. A. N., Chicoutimi and Tadoussac, writ returnable 1st September, 1854; Mr. Morin, appointed Judge of Superior Court 17th January, 1855.

Morin, L. S., Terrebonne, was elected on 23rd June, 1857, in room of G. M. Prevost, resigned.

Morrison, J. C., Niagara, **Town, appointed** Receiver General, 24th May, 1856; re-elected, 20th June, 1856.

Murney, E., Hastings, N. R., resigned **on** 15th September, 1856, with a view to being elected to Legislative Council.

Macdonald, Hon. J. A., Kingston, City, appointed Attorney General, U. C., 11th September, 1854; re-elected, 28th September, 1854.

McKerlie, D., Brant, E. R., declared to be duly elected, 12th March, 1855.

MacNab, Sir A. N. Knight, Hamilton, City, appointed President of Executive Council, 11th September, 1856; re-elected 2nd October, 1854.

Papin, J., L'Assomption, died on 23rd February, 1862.

Poulin, P. N., Rouville, resigned on 3rd September, 1856, with a view to offer as a Candidate for election to Legislative Council.

Prevost, G. M., Terrebonne, resigned on 29th May, 1857.

Price, D. E., Chicoutimi and Tadoussac, was elected on 26th April, 1855, in room of Hon. A. N. Morin, appointed Judge.

Sicotte, Hon. L. V., St. Hyacinthe, appointed Member of Executive Council and Commissioner of Crown Lands, 25th November, 1857.

Simard, G. H., Quebec, City, **was** elected on 27th October, 1856, in room of Hon. J. Chabot, appointed Judge.

Smith, Henry, Frontenac, appointed Solicitor General, U. C., on **11th** September, 1854; re-elected 28th September, 1854.

Spence, R., Wentworth, N. R., appointed Postmaster General, 11th September, 1854; re-elected 13th October, 1854.

Stuart, G. O., Quebec, City, elected on 14th April, 1857, in room of J. Blanchet, resigned.

Supple, J., Renfrew, was elected on 31st March, 1856, in room of Hon. F. Hincks, resigned.

Taché, J. C., Rimouski, resigned on 18th January, 1857.

Terrill, Hon. T. L., Stanstead, appointed Provincial Secretary on 24th May, 1856; re-elected 10th June, 1856.

Contested Elections, Special Elections, &c.- (Continued.)

## SIXTH PARLIAMENT.

### 13th January, 1858, to 10th June, 1861.

Abbott, J. J. C., Argenteuil, his name substituted for the name of S. Bellingham, as Member for Argenteuil, 12th March, 1860.

Allan, C., Wellington, N. R., his election declared null and void on 14th July, 1858; re-elected 23rd August, 1858.

Alleyn, C., Quebec, City, declared not duly elected, 16th April, 1860.
  " " (West), was elected on 7th May, 1860.

Bell, R., Lanark, N. R., resigned on 24th September, 1860; re-elected on 26th October, 1860.

Bellingham, S., Argenteuil. The name of J. J. C. Abbott is substituted for the name of S. Bellingham, 12th March, 1860.

Brown, Geo., Toronto City and N. R. Oxford, elects to serve for Toronto, 19th April, 1858; appointed Inspector General, 2nd August, 1858; re-elected 1st September, 1858.

Buchanan, I., Hamilton City, his resignation not accepted, 16th March, 1861.

Cameron, Hon. M., Lambton, resigned on 21st September, 1860.

Caron, L. B., L'Islet, his election declared null and void, 7th June, 1858.

Caron, Geo., Maskinongé, was elected on 14th December, 1858, in room of L. H. Gauvreau, deceased.

Cayley, Hon. W., **Renfrew, was elected on** 3rd March, 1858, in room of J. L. Macdougald, appointed Coroner.

Christie, D., Brant, E. R., resigned his **seat on** 4th October, 1858, to offer as candidate at election for Legislative Council.

Church, R. B., Leeds & Grenville, N. R., died in April, 1858.

Cimon, C., Charlevoix, Writ returnable 10th February, 1858.

Connor, N., Oxford, S. R., appointed Solicitor General, U. C., 2nd August, 1858; re-elected 7th September, 1858.

**Craik,** R., Middlesex, E. R., was elected on 31st May, 1860, **in room** of M. Talbot, deceased.

Dorion, Hon. A. A., Montreal City, appointed Commissioner of **Crown Lands** 2nd August, 1858; re-elected 9th September, 1858.

Drummond, Hon. L. T., Sherford, appointed Attorney-General, L. C., 2nd August, 1858; was elected for Lotbinière 2nd October, 1858; A. B. Foster, having been elected for Shefford, on 14th September, 1858.

Dubord, H., Quebec City, declared not duly elected, 16th April, 1860.

Fellows, G. B. L., Russell, his election declared fraudulent by Jury, at Assizes on 29th October, 1859; and verdict confirmed by Court in Toronto, on 2nd December, 1859. Mr. Fellows resigned his seat on 1st November, 1859; J. W. Loux was elected in his place on 21st December, 1859.

Finlayson, H., Brant, E. R., was elected on 1st December, 1858, in room of D. Christie, resigned.

Foley, Hon. M. H., Waterloo, N. R., appointed Postmaster-General, 2nd August, 1858; re-elected 23rd August, 1858.

Foster, A. B., Shefford, was elected on 14th September, 1858, in room of the Hon. L. T. Drummond; resigned his seat.

Fournier, C. F., L'Islet, declared duly elected, 7th June, 1858.

Galt, Hon. A. T., Sherbrooke, Town, appointed Inspector-General, 7th August, 1858; re-elected 23rd August, 858.

Gauvreau, L. H., Maskinongé, died on 30th October, 1858.

Gowan, O. R., Leeds and Grenville, N. R., was elected on 21st May, 1858, in room of B. R. Church, deceased.

Harcourt, M., Haldimand, was returned on 7th October, 1858, in room of W. L. Mackenzie resigned; was declared duly elected 19th April, 1861.

Hartman, J., York, N. R., died, 29th November, 1859; A. Wilson, elected in his room on 14th January, 1860.

Harwood, Hon. R. U., Vaudreuil, resigned on 3rd October, 1860; J. B. Mongenais was elected in his place, 26th November, 1860.

## Contested Elections, Special Elections, &c.-- (Continued.)

Huot, P. G., Quebec City, East, elected on 10th May, 1859; his resignation not accepted 10th March, 1861.

Laberge, C. J., Iberville, appointed Solicitor-General L. C., 2nd August, 1858; re-elected 6th September, 1858

LaRontillier, J., Gaspé, writ returnable on 10th February, 1858.

Lemieux, Hon. F., Levis, appointed Receiver-General, 2nd August, 1858; re-elected 20th August, 1858.

Loux, J. W., Russell, was elected on 21st December, 1859, in room of G. S. L. Fellowes.

Merritt, Hon. W. H., Lincoln, resigned his seat on 21st September, 1860, in order to be elected to Legislative Council; J. C. Rykert, elected in his room on 7th November, 1860.

Mongenais, J. B., Vaudreuil, was elected on 28th November, 1860, in the room of Hon. R. U. Harwood resigned.

Morin, Hon. L. S., Terrebonne, appointed Solicitor General, L. C., on 19th January, 1860; was re-elected on 21st February, 1860.

Mowat, Hon. O., Ontario, S. R., appointed Provincial Secretary, 2nd August, 1858; re-elected 4th September, 1858.

Macdonald, A. P., Middlesex, W. R., was elected on 5th August, 1858, in the room of J. Scatcherd, deceased.

Macdonald, Hon. J. S., Cornwall, Town, appointed Attorney General, U. C., 2nd August, 1858; re-elected 1st September, 1858.

Macdougald, J. L., Renfrew, appointed Coroner in February, 1858, Hon. W. Cayley, elected in his room on 3rd March, 1858.

McDougall, W., Oxford, N. R., was elected on 14th May, 1858, (see Brown, Geo.)

MacKenzie, W. L., Haldimand, resigned his seat on 16th August, 1858. Died on 28th August, 1861.

MacKenzie, H. F., Lambton, was elected on 19th November, 1860, in the room of Hon. M. Cameron, resigned.

O'Farrell, J., Lotbinière, expelled on 12th May, 1858. His Election declared null and void on 17th May, 1858.

Price, D. E., Chicoutimi and Saguenay. Writ returnable on 10th February, 1858.

Purdy, J. T., Grey, was elected on 4th March, 1861, in the room of J. S. Hogan, deceased.

Ross, D., Beauce, died in May, 1855.

Ross, Jas., Wellington, N. R., was elected on 23rd February, 1859, in room of Chs. Allan, deceased.

Rykert, J. C., Lincoln, was elected on 7th November, 1860, in room of Hon. W. H. Merritt, resigned.

Scatcherd, J., Middlesex, W. R., died on 15th June, 1858.

Sherwood, Hon. G., Brockville, Town, appointed Receiver General, 7th August, 1858; re-elected 2nd September, 1858.

Simard, G. H., Quebec City, declared not duly elected, 16th April, 1860.
"  Quebec City, (centre) was elected on 7th May, 1860.

Smith, Sidney, Northumberland, W. R., appointed Postmaster General, 2nd February, 1858; re-elected 22nd February, 1858.

Talbot, M., Middlesex, E. R. His decease reported on 26th March, 1858. R. Craik, elected in his room on 31st May, 1860.

Thibaudeau, Hon. J. E., Portneuf, appointed President of Executive Council, 2nd August, 1858; re-elected 11th September, 1858.

Wilson, A., York, N. R., was elected on 14th January, 1860, in room of J. Hartman, deceased.

## Contested Elections, Special Elections, &c.—(*Continued.*)

# SEVENTH PARLIAMENT.

### 15th *July*, 1861, *to* 16th *May*, 1863.

Abbott, Hon. J. J. C., Argenteuil, re-elected on 12th June, 1862, after his appointment as Solicitor General, L. C.

Benoit, P., Napierville, was elected on 17th November, 1862, in the room of Hon. J. O. Bureau, resigned.

Biggar, J. L., Northumberland, E. R., reported duly elected, 16th February, 1863.

Brown, Hon. Geo., Oxford, S. R., elected on 9th March, 1863, in the room of Hon. S. Connor, appointed Judge.

Bureau, Hon. J. O., Napierville, resigned on 15th September, 1862, with a view to offer as Candidate for Election to Legislative Council. P. Benoit elected in his room.

Carling, Hon. J., London City, re-elected on 7th April, 1862, after his appointment as Receiver General

Connor, Hon. S., Oxford, S. R., being appointed Judge, Hon. Geo. Brown was elected in his room.

Daly, T. M., Perth, was elected on 3rd July, 1862, in the room of Hon. M. H. Foley, resigned.

Dorion, Hon. A. A., Hochelaga, was elected on 20th June, 1862, in the room and place of J. P. Falkner, resigned.

Dorion, J. B. E., Drummond and Arthabaska, declared duly elected, 5th June, 1862.

Dufresne, J., Montcalm, was elected on 20th February, 1862, in the room of J. L. Martin, deceased.

Dunkin, C., Brome, elected 17th March, 1862, in the room of M. Sweet, appointed Postmaster of Warden.

Evanturel, Hon. F., Quebec, County, re-elected on 9th June, 1862, after his appointment as Minister of Agriculture.

Falkner, J. P., Hochelaga, resigned his seat on 6th June, 1862. Hon A. A. Dorion, elected in his room.

Foley, Hon. M. H., Perth, vacated his seat on being appointed Postmaster General. T. M. Daly was elected in his room, 3rd July, 1862.

Foley, Hon. M. H., Waterloo, N. R., was re-elected 9th June, 1862, after his appointment as Postmaster General.

Haultain, F. W., Peterborough, declared duly elected, 5th June, 1862.

Hooper, A. F., declared duly elected, 24th March, 1862.

Howland, Hon. W. P., York, W. R., was re-elected on 12th June, 1862, after his appointment as Receiver General.

Huntington, L. S., Shefford, declared duly elected, 31st May, 1862.

Kierskowski, A. E., Verchères, his election declared void, for want of proper qualification; C. F. Painchaud declared duly elected, 4th May, 1863

Labelle, P., Laval, appointed Inspector of Works, Hon. L. S. Morin elected in his room, 27th September, 1861.

Loranger, Hon. T. J. J., Laprairie, appointed Judge, A. Pinsonneault elected in his place.

Martin, J. L., Montcalm, died on 16th December, 1861.

Morin, Hon. L. S., Laval, was elected on 27th September, 1861, in the room of P. Labelle, appointed Inspector of Works.

Macbeth, G., Elgin, W. R., his election declared void, 23rd February, 1863.

Macdonald, Hon. J S., Cornwall, town, re-elected on 14th June, 1862, after his appointment as Attorney General, U. C.

**McDougall**, Hon. W., Oxford, N. R, declared duly elected, 15th April, 1863; re-elected on 14th June, 1862, after his appointment as Commissioner of Crown Lands.

McGee, **T. D.**, Montreal City, (West), declared duly elected, 3rd June, 1862.

O'Connor. J., Essex, was elected on 7th April, 1863, in the room of A. Rankin, whose election was declared void.

Painchaud, C. F., Verchères, declared duly elected, 4th May, 1863, in the room of A. E. Kierskowski, declared not qualified.

## Contested Elections, Special Elections, &c.—(Continued.)

Pinsonneault, A., Laprairie, elected on 1st April, 1863, in the room of Hon. T. J. J.
    Loranger, appointed Judge.
Rankin, A., Essex, his election declared void, 9th March, 1863.
Remillard, E., Bellechasse, declared duly elected, 5th June, 1862.
Robinson, Hon. J. B., Toronto City, (West), was re-elected on 23rd April, 1862, after his
    appointment as President of the Executive Council.
Scoble, J., Elgin, W. R., declared duly elected, 23rd February, 1863, in the room of G.
    Macbeth, whose election is declared void.
Sicotte, Hon. L. V., St. Hyacinthe, County, re-elected 12th June, 1862, after his appoint-
    ment as Attorney General, L. C.
Smith, J. S., Durham, E. R., his election declared void on 30th April, 1863.
Sweet, M., Brome, appointed Postmaster of Warden, C. Dunkin elected in his place,
    17th March, 1862.
Tett, B., Leeds, S. R., reported duly elected, 15th April, 1863.
Wilson, Hon. A., York, N. R., re-elected on 13th June, 1862, after his appointment as
    Solicitor General, U. C.

----

# EIGHTH PARLIAMENT.

### *3rd July,* 1863, *to* ——————

Beaubien, J. O., Montmagny, declared duly elected, 14th March, 1864.
Bell, R., Lanark, N. R., resigned his seat on 7th October, 1864, Hon. W. McDougall was
    elected in his place on 4th November, 1864.
Bell, R., Russell, declared duly elected, 23rd January, 1865.
Boucher de Niverville, Charles, Three Rivers, City, was elected on 16th January,
    1865, in room of Hon. J. E. Turcotte, deceased.
Bowman, J. E., Waterloo, N. R., was elected on 26th April, 1864, in room of Hon. M. H.
    Foley, who vacated his seat by his appointment as Postmaster General; Mr.
    Bowman's election confirmed, 30th August, 1865.
Brown, Hon. Geo., Oxford, S. R., was re-elected on 11th July 1864, after his appointment
    as President of the Executive Council.
Buchanan, Hon. I., Hamilton, City, re-elected, 20th April, 1864, after his appointment as
    President of the Executive Council; reported duly elected, 25th January, 1865;
    resigned his seat on 17th January, 1865. Chs. Magill elected in his place.
Cameron, M. C., Ontario, N. R., was elected on 30th July, 1864, in the room of Hon.
    W. McDougall, who vacated his seat by his appointment as Provincial Secretary.
Cartier, Hon. G. E., Montreal City, East, declared duly elected 15th March, 1864;
    re-elected 11th April, 1864, after his appointment as Attorney General, L. C.
Chambers, F. H., Brockville, Town, reported duly elected, 2nd February, 1863.
Chapais, Hon. J. C., Kamouraska, was re-elected on 14th April, 1864, after his appoint-
    ment as Commissioner of Public Works.
Cockburn, Hon. J., Northumberland, W. R., was re-elected on 23rd April, 1864, after his
    appointment as Solicitor General, U. C.
Cornellier dit Grandchamps, H. Joliette, declared duly elected, 30th January, 1863.
De Niverville, Boucher, C., Three Rivers, City, was elected on 16th January, 1865, in
    room of Hon. J. E. Turcotte, deceased.
Dorion, Hon. A A., Hochelaga, declared duly elected, 22nd March, 1864.
Foley, Hon. M. H., Waterloo, N. R., vacated his seat by his appointment as Postmaster
    General; J. E. Bowman was elected in his place on 26th April, 1864.
Galt, Hon. A. T., Sherbrooke, Town, was re-elected on 11th April, 1864, after his appoint-
    ment as Minister of Finance.
Gaucher, G. G., Jacques Cartier, was elected on 26th August, 1864, in the room of T. J.
    Tassé appointed Inspector of Prisons.
Geoffrion, F., Verchères, declared duly elected, 17th May, 1864.

## Contested Elections, Special Elections, &c.—(*Continued.*)

Gibbs, T. N., Ontario, S. R., was elected on 18th January, 1865, in room of Hon. O. Mowat, appointed Vice-Chancellor.

Haultain, F. W., Peterborough, was elected on 14th September, 1864, in room of W. S Conger, deceased

Howland, Hon. W. P., York, W. R., was re-elected on 14th December, 1864, after his appointment as Postmaster General.

Irvine, G., Megantic, declared duly elected, 2nd October, 1863.

Jones, D. F., Leeds, S. R., was elected on 30th January, 1864, in the room of Hon. A. N. Richards, who vacated his seat by accepting the office of Solicitor General, U C.

Labreche Viger, L., Terrebonne, declared duly elected, 16th June, 1864

Laframboise, Hon. M , Bagot, was re-elected on 15th August, 1863, after his appointment as Commissioner of Public Works.

Langevin, Hon. H. L., Dorchester, was re elected on 11th April, 1864, after his appointment as Sol citor General for L. C.

Macdonald, Hon. J. A., Kingston City, was re-elected on 11th April, 1864, after his re-appointment as Attorney General, U. C.

McDougall, Hon. W., Ontario, N. R., having vacated his seat by accepting the office of Provincial Secretary, M. C. Cameron was elected in his place on 30th July, 1864, Mr McDougall was elected for N. R. Lanark, on 4th November, 1864

McGee, Hon. T. D , Montreal City, (West), was re-elected on 11th April, 1864, after his appointment as Minister of Agriculture.

McMonies, J., Wentworth, N. R., was elected in the room of W. Notman, deceased.

Magill, Charles, Hamilton City, was elected on 21st February, 1865, in the room of Hon. I. Buchanan, resigned.

Morrison, A., Niagara, Town, was elected on 7th September, 1864, in room of Hon. J. Simpson, appointed Assistant Auditor.

Mow t, Hon. O., Ontario, S. R , was re-elected on 18th July, 1864, after his appointment as Postmaster General ; was appointed Vice Chancellor, on 14th November, 1864.

Notman, W., Wentworth, N. R., died in September, 1865.

Perreault, J. F., Richelieu, declared duly elected, 25th January, 1865.

Pissonneault, A., Laprairie, declared duly elected 4th March, 1864.

Powell W. F., Carleton, declared duly elected 21st March, 1864.

Price, D. E., Chicoutimi and Saguenay, resigned on 4th October, 1864, with a view to being elected to Legislative Council.

Rankin A., Essex, his name inserted on 17th M y, 1864, in the return of the Returning Officer, by order of the House, as member elected for the county of Essex.

Raymond R., St. Hyacinthe, was elected on 1st October, 1863, in the room of Hon. L. V. Sicotte, appointed Judge.

Remillard, E., Bellechasse, declared duly elected, 11th May, 1864.

Richards, Hon A. N., Leeds, S. R., vacated his seat by accepting the office of Solicitor General, U C. on 26th December, 1863. D. F. Jones was elected in his place on 30th January, 1864.

Sicotte Hon. L. V. St. Hyacinthe, was appointed Judge of the Superior Court on 5th September, 1863

Simpson, Hon. J., Niagara, Town, was re-elected on 11th April, 1864, after his appointment as Provincial Secretary ; was appointed Assistant Auditor of Public Accounts on 13th August, 1864. A. Morrison, was elected in his room on 7th September, 1864.

Tassé, T. Z., Jacques Cartier, having been appointed Inspector of Prisons, G. G. Gaucher, was elected in his place on 26th August, 1864.

Tremblay, P. A. Chicoutimi and Saguenay, was elected on 3rd January, 1865, in the room of D. E. Price, resigned.

Turcotte, Hon. J. E., Three Rivers, City, died on 20th December, 1864. C Boucher de Niverville was elected in his room on 16th January, 1865.

**Wright, Alonzo,** Ottawa, County, declared duly elected 3rd June, 1864.

## Contested Elections, Special Elections, &c.—(Continued.)

Number of appointments to Executive Council, from 1841 to 1865, inclusive ...... 132
    Of whom are French Canadians ..... 44
Number of appointments to Legislative Council, from 1841 to 1856, inclusive ..... ●
    Of whom are French Canadians ..... 24
Elections to Legislative Council, from 1856 to 1865, inclusive ............... 39
    Of whom are French Canadians ..... 27
Elections to Legislative Assembly, from 1841 to 1865, inclusive ..... ●
    Of whom are French Canadians .... 321
Appointment to secondary offices in Executive and Legislative Departments, from
    1841 to 1865, inclusive ............................... ●
    Of whom are French Canadians ..... 30
Appointments to the Bench, L. C ....................................... 64
    Of whom are French Canadians ..... 32
Appointments to the Bench, U. C. ..................................... ●

## Special Council, Lower Canada.

## From 1838 to 1840.

### Members of the Special Council.

Hon. Jas. Cuthbert.
  " T. Pothier.
  " C. E. C. DeLery.
  " James Stuart.
  " P. McGill.
  " M. P. De Sales Laterrière.
  " B. Joliette.
  " P. De Rocheblave.
  " John Neilson.
  " A. Dionne.
  " S. Gerrard.
  " Jules Quesnel.
  " W. P. Christie.
  " Chs. E. Casgrain.
  " Wm. Walker.
  " Jos. E. Faribault.
  " John Molson.
  " E. Mayrand.

Hon. P. H. Knowlton.
  " T. Penn.
  " Jos. Dionne.
  " I. Smith.
  " Geo. Moffatt.
  " R. U. Harwood.
  " E. Hale, of Sherbrooke.
  " J. Wainwright.
  " E. Hale, of Portneuf.
  " C. R. Ogden.
  " D. Daly.
  " F. G. Heriot.
  " T. Austin.
  " H. Black.
  " D. Mondelet.
  " C. D. Day.
  " J. B. Taché.

## Court of Queen's Bench (Superior Court), Lower Canada.
### From 1841 to 1849 inclusive.

| JUDGES. | FROM | TO |
|---|---|---|
| *Chief Justices.* | | |
| Sir Jas. Stuart, Bart.......... | 10th February, 1841, | 31st December, 1849. |
| J. R. Vallières de St. Réal, Montreal.............. | 1st June, 1842, | 17th February, 1847. |
| J. R. Rolland, Montreal........ | 23rd April, 1847, | 31st December, 1849. |
| *Puisné Judges.* | | |
| Edwd. Bowen, Quebec........ | 10th February, 1841, | " |
| Phi. Panet, " ........ | " | " |
| Elz. Bédard, " ........ | " | 25th April, 1848. |
| T. C. Aylwin, " ........ | 26th April, 1848, | 31st December, 1849. |
| Geo. Pyke, Montreal......... | 10th February, 1841, | 28th June, 1842. |
| J. R. Rolland, " ........ | " | 22nd April, 1847. |
| Saml. Gale, " ........ | " | 25th April, 1848. |
| C. D. Day, " ........ | 29th June, 1842, | 31st December, 1849. |
| Jas. Smith, " ........ | 23rd April, 1847, | " |
| Elz. Bédard, " ........ | 26th April, 1848, | 11th August, 1849. |
| J. R. Vallières de St. Réal, Three Rivers.................. | 10th February, 1841, | 31st May, 1842. |
| D. Mondelet, Three Rivers..... | 1st June, 1842, | 31st December, 1849. |
| J. Fletcher, St. Francis........ | 10th February, 1841, | 11th October, 1844. |
| B. H. Gairdner, " ........ | 11th November, 1844, | 31st December, 1849. |
| J. G. Thompson, Gaspé........ | 10th February, 1841, | 30th September, 1849. |
| E. H. Bowen, " ........ | 1st October, 1847, | 31st March, 1849. |

## Court of Queen's Bench (Appeal and Criminal), Lower Canada.
### From 1850 to 1865 inclusive.

| JUDGES. | FROM | TO |
|---|---|---|
| *Chief Justices.* | | |
| Sir Jas. Stuart, Bart.......... | 1st January, 1850, | Died 14th July, 1853. |
| Sir L. H. LaFontaine, Bart..... | 13th August, 1853, | Died 26th Feby., 1864. |
| Hon. J. F. J. Duval.......... | 5 March, 1864, | |
| *Puisné Judges.* | | |
| Hon. J. R. Rolland.......... | 1st January, 1850, | 26th January, 1855. |
| " Phi. Panet ............ | " | Died 15th Jany., 1855. |
| " T. C. Aylwin............ | " | |
| " J. F. J. Duval.......... | 27th January, 1855, | 4th March, 1864. |
| " R. E. Caron............ | " | |
| " W. C. Meredith.......... | 12th March, 1859. | |
| " W. Badgley, Asst. Judge.. | 12th September, 1863, | 31st December, 1864. |
| " L. T. Drummond, Puisné J. | 5th March, 1864, | |
| " C. J. E. Mondelet, A. Jud. | 1st January, 1865, | |

# Superior Court, Lower Canada.

## From 1850 to 1865 inclusive.

| JUDGES. | FROM | TO |
|---|---|---|
| Hon. Edw. Bowen, Chf. Justice. | 1st January, 1850, | Died 11th April, 1866. |
| " D. Mondelet, Puisné Judg. | " | Died in 1863. |
| " C. D. Day, " .. | " | 30th September, 1862. |
| " Jas. Smith, " .. | " | |
| " Geo. Vanfelson, " .. | " | 26th January, 1856. |
| " R. H. Gairdner, " .. | " | 30th September, 1852. |
| " E. Bacquet, " .. | 1st January, 1852, | Died in 1852. |
| " C. J. E. Mondelet, " .. | " | 31st December, 1864. |
| " J. F. Duval, " .. | " | 26th January, 1855. |
| " W. C. Meredith, " .. | " | 11th March, 1859. |
| " E. Short, " .. | 12th November, 1852, | |
| " R. E. Caron, " .. | 15th August, 1853, | 26th January, 1855. |
| " A. N. Morin, " .. | 27th January, 1855, | Died 27th July, 1865. |
| " W. Badgley, " .. | " | 11th September, 1863. |
| " J. Chabot, " .. | 20th September, 1856, | Died in 1860. |
| " Hyp. Guy, " .. | 25th November, 1857, | 10th April, 1860. |
| " J. S. McCord, " .. | " | March, 1865. |
| " W. K. McCord, " .. | " | 1856. |
| " W. Power, " .. | " | Died in 1860. |
| " J. C. Bruneau, " .. | " | 4th September, 1863. |
| " J. A. Taschereau, " .. | " | |
| " D. Roy, " .. | " | |
| " P. Winter, " .. | 29th March, 1858, | |
| " J. T. Taschereau, Asst. J. | 2nd November, 1858, | 2nd May, 1859. |
| " " | 6th June, 1860, | August, 1865. |
| " " Puisné Judge | — August, 1865. | |
| " A. Stuart, Asst. Judge. | 10th February, 1859, | 6th June, 1860. |
| " " Puisné Judge.. | 6th June, 1860, | |
| " J. A. Berthelot, Asst. J... | 10th February, 1859, | 31st December, 1864, |
| " " Puisné Judge. | 1st January, 1865, | |
| " J. G. Thompson, " | 11th May, 1859, | |
| " A. Lafontaine, " | " | |
| " S. C. Monk, Asst. Judge.. | 4th June, 1859, | |
| " A. Polette, Puisné Judge. | 21st April, 1860, | |
| " F. O. Gauthier, " | 14th November, 1860, | |
| " T. J. J. Loranger, " | 28th February, 1863, | |
| " L. V. Sicotte, " | 5th September, 1863, | |
| " C. J. Laberge, " | 18th September, 1863, | 2nd July, 1864. |
| " F. G. Johnson, " | 1st June, 1865, | |

*Deputy Judges, Superior Court.*

| | | |
|---|---|---|
| J. B. Parkin..................... | 22nd December, 1854, | 11th May, 1855. |
| Chs. Panet..................... | 16th May, 1855, | 8th July, 1855. |
| J. J. C. Abbott............... | 19th May, 1855. | 25th August, 1855. |

## Superior Court, Lower Canada—(*Continued.*)

| JUDGES. | FROM | TO |
|---|---|---|
| *Asst. Judges under Seigniorial Act.* | | |
| H. Driscoll...................... | 3rd September, 1855, | |
| G. O. Stuart.................... | " | |
| F. O. Gauthier................. | " | |
| J. T. Taschereau.............. | " | |
| J. B. Parkin.................... | " | |
| S. C. Monk .................... | 14th September, 1855, | |
| J. F. Pelletier................. | " | |
| J. A. Berthelot ............... | " | |

## Court of Vice-Admiralty (Quebec.)

### From 1841 to 1865.

| | | |
|---|---|---|
| Hon. H. Black, Judge......... | 10th February, 1841, | ———————— |

## Court of Queen's Bench, Upper Canada.

### 1841 to 1865.

| JUDGES. | FROM | TO |
|---|---|---|
| *Chief Justices.* | | |
| Sir J. B. Robinson, Bart....... | 10th February, 1841, | 14th March, 1862. |
| Hon. A. McLean.............. | 15th March, 1862, | 21st July, 1863. |
| " W. H. Draper, C. B...... | 22nd July, 1863, | — |
| *Puisné Judges.* | | |
| Hon. J. B. Macaulay.......... | 10th February, 1841, | 14th December, 1849. |
| " A. McLean.............. | " | 31st December, 1849. |
| " J. Jones................ | " | 30th July, 1848. |
| " C. A. Hagerman......... | " | 12th May, 1847. |
| " W. H. Draper........... | 12th June, 1847, | 4th February, 1856. |
| " R. B. Sullivan.......... | 15th September, 1848, | 31st December, 1849. |
| " A. McLean ............. | 5th February, 1856, | 14 March, 1862. |
| " R. E. Burns............. | 21st January, 1850, | Died in January, 1863. |
| " J. H. Hagarty........... | 18th March, 1862, | |
| " S. Connor........:...... | 31st January, 1863, | Died 29th April, 1863. |
| " A. Wilson.............. | 11th May, 1863, | 23rd August, 1863. |
| " J. C. Morrison.......... | 24th August, 1863, | |

## Court of Common Pleas, Upper Canada.

### 1841 to 1865.

| JUDGES. | FROM | TO |
|---|---|---|
| *Chief Justices.* | | |
| Hon. J. B. Macaulay, Knight... | 1st January, 1850, | 4th February, 1856. |
| " W. H. Draper, C. B...... | 5th February, 1856, | 21st July, 1863. |
| " W. B. Richards......... | 22nd July, 1863, | |
| *Puisné Judges.* | | |
| Hon. A. McLean............ | 1st January, 1850, | 4th February, 1856. |
| " R. B. Sullivan........... | " | 14th April, 1852. |
| " W. B. Richards......... | 22nd June, 1853. | 21st July, 1863. |
| " J. H. Hagarty........... | 5th February, 1856, | 17th March, 1862. |
| " J. C. Morrison........... | 18th March, 1862, | 23rd August, 1863. |
| " A. Wilson............... | 24th August, 1863, | |
| " Jos. Wilson............. | 22nd July, 1863. | |

## Court of Chancery, Upper Canada.

| NAMES. | FROM | TO |
|---|---|---|
| *Chancellors.* | | |
| Hon. W. H. Blake.......... | 1st January, 1850, | 18th March, 1862. |
| " P. M. Vankoughnet...... | 18th March, 1862, | |
| *Vice Chancellors.* | | |
| Hon. R. S. Jameison.......... | 10th February, 1841, | 31st December, 1849. |
| " J. P. C. Esten........... | 1st January, 1850, | 24th October, 1864. |
| " J. G. Spragge........... | 1st January, 1851, | |
| " O. Mowat............... | 14th November, 1864. | |

## (1) Court of Error and Appeal, Upper Canada.

| | | |
|---|---|---|
| *Presiding Judge.* | | |
| Hon. A. McLean.............. | 1st January, 1864. | Died 24th Oct., 1865. |

(1) This Court is composed of the Judges for the time being of the Court of Queen's Bench, the Court of Chancery and the Court of Common Pleas, and, prior to 1st January, 1864, was presided over by the Chief Justice of the Court of Queen's Bench.

### Pensions granted to Judges of Superior Courts, Lower Canada.

### From 1841 to 1865.

| NAMES. | FROM | TO |
|---|---|---|
| Hon. Jas. Reid, Chief Justice, Montreal............... | 10th February, 1841, | 19th January, 1848. |
| Hon. Geo. Pyke, Puisné Judge, Montreal................ | 29th June, 1842, | 3rd February, 1851. |
| Hon. Saml. Gale, Puisné Judge, Montreal......... ....... | 26th April, 1848, | ———— |
| Hon. J. R. Rolland, Chief Justice, Montreal................ | 27th January, 1855, | Died 5th August, 1862. |
| Hon. C. D. Day, Puisné Judge, Montreal................ | 1st October, 1862, | ———— |
| Hon. J. C. Bruneau, Puisné Judge, Montreal.......... | 5th September, 1863, | ———— |
| Widow of late Justice Fletcher, St. Francis............... | 12th October, 1844, | Died 13th Mar., 1848. |
| Widow of Chief Justice Vallières, Montreal........... | 28th July, 1847. | ———— |
| Widow of Judge Bédard, Montreal ..................... | 12th August, 1849, | ———— |

### Pensions granted to Judges of Superior Courts, Upper Canada.

### 1841 to 1865.

| NAMES. | FROM | TO |
|---|---|---|
| Hon. L. P. Sherwood, Puisné Judge.................. | 10th February, 1841, | 19th May, 1850. |
| Hon. J. B. Macaulay, Chief Justice, C. P............... | 5th February, 1856 | 26th November, 1859. |
| Sir J. B. Robinson, Chief Justice, Q. B................. | 15th March, 1862, | Died 31st Jany., 1863. |
| Hon. W. H. Blake, Chancellor.. | 19th March, 1862, | ———— |
| Hon. A. McLean, Chief Justice, Queen's Bench ............ | 22nd July, 1863, | Died 24th Oct., 1865. |

## Queen's Counsel, Lower Canada.

### 1841 to 1865 inclusive.

| NAMES. | | NAMES. | |
|---|---|---|---|
| F. W. Primrose | 1842 | F. Lemieux | 1854 |
| C. S. Cherrier | " | T. L. Terrill | " |
| D. Fisher | " | T. J. J. Loranger | " |
| C. R. Ogden | " | Chs. Panet | 1855 |
| L. H. LaFontaine | " | Jas. Hallowell | " |
| T. C. Aylwin | " | F. Griffin, (precedence) | 1856 |
| A. N. Morin | " | C. Alleyn | 1857 |
| W. C. Meredith | 1844 | C. J. Laberge | 1858 |
| J. R. Hamilton | " | J. A. Berthelot | 1859 |
| J. A. Taschereau | 1845 | J. T. Taschereau | 1860 |
| W. Badgley | 1847 | F. O. Gauthier | " |
| W. K. McCord | " | E. Carter | 1862 |
| J. E. Turcotte | " | J. J. C. Abbott | " |
| J. Duval | 1848 | A. A. Dorion | 1863 |
| F. G. Johnson | " | L. S. Huntington | " |
| John Rose | " | F. Andrews | " |
| R. E. Caron | " | J. J. Day | " |
| L. T. Drummond | " | L. G. Baillargé | " |
| P. B. Dumoulin | 1853 | J. B. Parkin | " |
| F. G. Johnson | " | Hy. Stuart | " |
| John Rose | " | U. J. Tessier | " |
| P. J. O. Chauveau | " | T. Fournier | " |
| Dunbar Ross | " | J. S. Sanborn | " |
| A. Polette | 1854 | J. Doutre | " |
| Hy. H. Judah | " | F. Cassidy | ● |
| G. O. Stuart | " | R. Laflamme | ● |
| F. Griffin | " | S. Bethune | 1864 |
| G. W. Wicksteed | " | A. Cross | " |
| N. F. Belleau | " | C. G. Holt | ● |
| J. Chabot | " | J. M. Hudon | ● |
| A. Stuart | " | S. Lelièvre | " |
| W. L. Felton | " | J. O'Halloran | " |
| N. Dumas | " | L. A. Olivier | " |
| G. E. Cartier | " | A. Robertson | " |
| S. C. Monk | " | R. Roy | " |
| L. V. Sicotte | " | H. L. Langevin | " |

## Queen's Counsel, Upper Canada.

### From 1841 to 1865 inclusive.

| NAMES. | | NAMES. | |
|---|---|---|---|
| W. H. Draper | 1842 | R. Macdonald | 1856 |
| H. J. Boulton | " | G. Sherwood | " |
| R. Baldwin | " | Jas. Smith | " |
| H. Sherwood, (precedence) | " | John Wilson | " |
| J. E. Small | " | L. Wallbridge | " |
| S. B. Harrison | 1845 | G. B. L. Fellowes | " |
| J. H. Cameron | 1846 | S. B. Freeman | " |
| J. A. Macdonald | " | H. C. R. Becher | " |
| Hy. Smith | " | Hy. Eccles | " |
| T. Kirkpatrick | " | A. Campbell | " |
| R. B. Sullivan | " | S. Brough | 1858 |
| W. H. Blake | 1848 | J. Duggan | " |
| J. S. Macdonald | 1849 | S. B. Richards | " |
| T. M. Radenhurst | 1850 | T. Galt | " |
| W. Notman | " | D. B. Read | " |
| J. W. Gwynne | " | J. Patton | 1862 |
| W. B. Richards | " | Sidney Smith | " |
| A. Wilson | " | J. Bell | 1863 |
| John Ross | " | J. Hector | " |
| J. H. Hagarty | " | G. W. Burton | " |
| S. Connor | " | J. Cockburn | " |
| P. M. Vankoughnet | " | A. N. Richards | " |
| J. Prince | 1852 | S. H. Strong | " |
| J. C. Morrison | 1853 | M. C. Cameron | " |
| K. Mackenzie | " | Æ. Irving | " |
| O. Mowat | 1856 | G. Robinson | " |
| J. B. Macaulay | " | A. Crooks | " |
| M. O'Reilly | " | J. O'Reilly | 1864 |

### Revised Statutes, Lower Canada.

| NAMES. | FROM | TO |
|---|---|---|
| *Commissioners for the Revision.* | | |
| A. Buchanan | 16th March, 1842. | 1st July, 1845. |
| H. Heney | " | Died on —— |
| G. W. Wicksteed | " | 1st July, 1845. |

### Revised Statutes, Upper Canada.

| *Commissioners of Revision.* | | |
|---|---|---|
| J. B. Robinson | 25th July, 1840, | |
| J. B. Macaulay | " | |
| W. H. Draper | " | |
| J. H. Cameron | " | |

## Consolidated Statutes, Upper Canada.

| NAMES. | FROM | TO |
|---|---|---|
| *Commission for Consolidation.* | | |
| Hon. J. H. Cameron.............. | 7th February, 1856. | 26th January, 1857. |
| J. C. Morrison.................. | " | 19th December, 1856. |
| Adam Wilson................... | " | |
| S. Connor..................... | " | |
| O. Mowat..................... | " | |
| D. B. Read................... | " | 5th December, 1859. |
| S. H. Strong, in the room of J. C. Morrison, resigned...... | 20th December, 1856, | " |
| Hon. J. B. Macaulay, in the stead of Hon. J. H. Cameron, re-signed................... | 27th January, 1857, | " |
| Judge Gowan ............... | 3rd November, 1859, | " |

## Consolidated Statutes, Lower Canada.

| NAMES. | FROM | TO |
|---|---|---|
| *Commission for Consolidation.* | | |
| A. Polette................... | 28th March, 1856, | 31st January, 1861. |
| G. W. Wicksteed............. | " | " |
| Andrew Stuart .............. | " | " |
| Ths. J. J. Loranger......... | " | " |
| R. McKay .................. | " | " |
| G. DeBoucherville........... | " | " |

## Consolidated Statutes, Canada.

| NAMES. | FROM | TO |
|---|---|---|
| *Commissioners for Consolidation.* | | |
| The Commissioners for the Consolidation of the Public General Statutes of Lower Canada and Upper Canada respectively, were further appointed in jointly for the Consolidation of the Public General Statutes of Canada | Feby. and Mar., 1856, | 5th December, 1859. |

## Codification of the Civil Law in Lower Canada, under Act 20 Vic. ch. 43.

| NAMES. | FROM | TO |
|---|---|---|
| *Commissioners for Codification.* | | |
| Hon. R. E. Caron .............. | —— February, 1859, | |
| " C. D. Day................. | " | |
| " A. N. Morin............. | " | Died 27th July, 18 |
| J. U. Beaudry................ | 7th August, 1865, | |

## Foreign Consuls in Canada.

| Foreign Countries | Names of Consuls. | For what place. | When appointe |
|---|---|---|---|
| United States.... | C. Dorwin, Consul................... | " ....... | } prior to 1856 |
| " | ∴ Hon. J. R. Giddings, Consul General.... | B. N. America | 1862 |
| " | .... J. W. Howes, Vice Consul ... ........ | Montreal ...... | 1863 |
| " | ... Hon. J. F. Potter, Consul General..... | B. N. America | 1864 |
| " | ... C. S. Ogden, Consul............. | Quebec ..... | 1861 |
| " | ... D. Thurston, " | " | 1864 |
| " | ... W. H. F. Gurley, " | " | |
| " | ... D. Thurston, Consular Agent.......... | Toronto ...... | |
| " | ... R. J. Kimball, " | " | |
| " | .... J. W. Stoakes, " | Kingston........ | 1861 |
| " | .... J. C. Clark, " .......... | " | 1862 |
| " | ... S. B. Hanse, Consul............... | " | 1864 |
| " | .... I. D. Irvine, Consular Agent ........ | Hamilton ..... | 1861 |
| " | ... S. Heoman, " | Brockville ...... | |
| " | .. J. Harris, " | Clifton ........ | 1861 |
| " | ... A. A. Porter, Consul ............. | " ........ | 1864 |
| " | .... Geo. Perry, Consular Agent ........ | Cobourg ...... | |
| " | .... J. C. Kirkpatrick, " | Dunnville ..... | |
| " | ... J Douglas, " | Fort Erie...... | |
| " | .... F. N. Blake, Consul ............. | " | |
| " | ... E. Mill, Consular Agent .......... | Morpeth ...... | 1862 |
| " | ... R. O. Lake, " | Port Burwell .. | |
| " | ... J. Fortier, " | Port Colborne .. | |
| " | ... J. Albro, " | Port Hope..... | |
| " | ... W. H. Stephenson, " | Port Rowan ... | |
| " | ... R. C. McMullen, " | Port Sarnia.... | |
| " | ... A. Hendrick, Consul ............. | " | |
| " | ....J. L. Near, " | " " | 1865 |
| " | ... J. Bostwick, Consular Agent ........ | Port Stanley | |
| " | ... J. S. Hawley, " | Prescott ..... | |
| " | ... Jas. Weldon, " | " ........ | 1864 |
| " | ... D. C. Haynes, " | St. Catherines .. | |
| " | .... D. Munger, " | Windsor ...... | |
| " | .... J. W. Moore, " | " | |
| " | ... D. K. Hobart, Consul............. | " ........ | 1864 |
| " | ... W. Bennett, Consular Agent ........ | Point St. Charles | |
| " | .... E Fenessy, " | Coaticook........ | 1862 |
| " | .... C. H Powers, Consul ........... | " ....... | 1865 |

## Foreign Consuls in Canada—(Continued.)

| Foreign Countries | Names of Consuls. | For what place. | When appointed |
|---|---|---|---|
| United States | J. M. McMillan, Consular Agent | Dundee | |
| " | T. Fitnam, Consul | Gaspé Basin | 1864 |
| " | G. E. Berwick, Consular Agent | Herringford | |
| " | F. Myers, " | Lacolle | 1862 |
| " | W. H. Huestis, " | Longueuil & St. Lambert | 1864 |
| " | G. T. Moorehouse, " | St. Johns | |
| " | J. W. Buxter, " | Stanstead | |
| France | Thos. Ryan, Consul | Montreal | |
| " | Edw. Ryan, " | Quebec | |
| " | Baron Gauldrée Boilleau, Consul | " | 1859 |
| " | " Consul General | " | 1862 |
| " | T. Doucet, Consular Agent | Montreal | 1861 |
| " | W. J. Macdonell, " | Toronto | 1862 |
| " | A. F. Gauthier, Consul General | Canada | 1864 |
| Prussia | H. Chapman, Consul | Montreal | 1861 |
| " | G. Lomer, " | " | 1865 |
| Denmark | Ths. Ryan, " | " | prior to 1860 |
| " | A. Rimmer, " | " | 1863 |
| Sardinia, (Italy) | H. Chapman, " | " | 1861 |
| " | H. Leflontillier, " | Gaspé | 1862 |
| Spain | H. Chapman, " | Montreal | 1861 |
| Sweden & Norway | H. Chapman, Vice Consul | " | 1858 |
| " | A. Falkenberg, " | Quebec | 1854 |
| " | J. E. Barry, " | Escoumains | 1862 |
| Belgium | Jesse Joseph, Consul | Montreal | prior to 1856 |
| Portugal | C. S. Watson, Vice Consul | Montreal | 1863 |
| " | C. H. E. Tilstone, " | Quebec | 1863 |
| " | P. Vibert, " | Gaspé | 1863 |
| Hanover | H. Chapman, Consul | Montreal | 1851 |
| Lubeck | E. Ryan, " | Quebec | 1855 |
| " | G. T. Pemberton, " | " | 1864 |
| " | Ths. Ryan, " | Montreal | 1855 |
| Netherlands | B. H. Dixon, Consul General | Toronto | 1863 |
| Bremen | Ths. Ryan, Consul | Montreal | 1861 |
| " | G. A. Beling, " | Lower Canada | 1862 |
| Hamburg | Ths. Ryan, " | Montreal | 1861 |
| " | Ths. Ryan, " | Quebec | 1863 |
| Mecklemburg | G. Beling, " | " | 1862 |
| Uruguay | J. M. Grant, Vice Consul | Montreal | prior to 1856 |

# Royal Visits to Canada.

His Royal Highness **Prince William Henry**, subsequently King William IV. and uncle of Her Majesty, Queen Victoria, landed at Quebec in 1787.

H. R. H. **Prince Edward**, Duke of Kent, father of Queen Victoria, 1791.

H. R. H. Albert Edward, **Prince of Wales**, son of Queen Victoria, **1860.**

H. R. H. **Prince Alfred**, brother of the Prince of Wales, 1861.

H. R. H. **Prince de Joinville**, son of Louis Philippe, late King of **the** French, 1861.

**Prince Napoleon Bonaparte**, cousin of Napoleon III, Emperor of the French, 1861.

## CANADIANS HOLDING **TITLES OF HONOUR** UNDER THE BRITISH CROWN.

#### *Baronets :*

**Sir James Stuart**, late Chief Justice, Lower Canada.

**Sir A. N. MacNab**, late Prime Minister.

**Sir L. H. LaFontaine**, late Chief Justice, Lower Canada.

**Sir J. B. Robinson**, late Chief Justice, Upper Canada.

#### *Knights :*

**Sir David Jones.**

**Sir E. P. Taché**, late Minister of Militia.

**Sir A. N. MacNab**, late Prime Minister.

**Sir J. B. Macaulay, late** Chief Justice of Common Pleas, U. **C.**

**Sir W. E. Logan**, Provincial Geologist.

**Sir N. F. Belleau**, Premier of Administration of 1865.

**Sir Henry Smith**, late Speaker of Legislative Assembly.

#### *Companions of the Bath :*

**Hon. C. M. DeSalaberry**, late Lieut. Colonel Commanding the *Voltigeurs Canadiens* in 1812.

**Hon. Henry** Black, Judge of Vice-Admiralty **Court**, Quebec.

**Hon. T. E.** Campbell, late M. P. for Rouville.

**Hon. R.** Baldwin, late Attorney General, U. C.

**Hon. W. H.** Draper, Chief Justice of Upper Canada.

www.ingramcontent.com/pod-product-compliance
Lightning Source LLC
Chambersburg PA
CBHW030606270326
41927CB00007B/1068